The New Babel

The New Babel

Toward a Poetics of the Mid-East Crises

Leonard Schwartz

The University of Arkansas Press

FAYETTEVILLE

2016

CONTENTS

ACKNOWLEDGMENTS

Some of these poems and essays originally appeared with *Counterpunch, Search for a Common Ground News Service, The Denver Quarterly, Gallerie International* (Mumbai, India), *Harper's Magazine, Intervalles* (Belgium), *Jewish Daily Forward, Quarterly Review of Literature Singapore, Raintaxi,* and *26.* Other pieces appeared in three publications: *Language as Responsibility* (Tinfish), *The Tower of Diverse Shores,* and *Ear and Ethos* (Talisman House). I want to thank these various editors and publishers for their openness to form. A special thanks goes to Edward Foster for his steadfast support of the work. I am grateful to Susan Schultz, too, for her interest in these issues. A big debt of gratitude goes to Zohra Saed for her early support of this manuscript, and her introduction of it to the University of Arkansas Press. Thanks to Ruth Brownstein and John Ford at KAOS 89.3 FM Olympia for their support of the radio program all these years, and to Holly Melgard, Zoe Ward, and Claire Sammons for their transcriptions of the interviews in this book. Thanks, too, to Michael Bieker of the University of Arkansas Press for taking an interest, David Scott Cunningham for his fine editorial steering, and Deena Owens for invaluable help in manuscript preparation. Thank you to Brian King for his dedicated and absolutely essential copy editing and all around improvement of certain texts, and to Melissa King for her savvy maneuvers in making this book ready for the world. To my spouse, Zhang Er, many thanks go as well, for her abiding companionship throughout.

INTRODUCTION

Poetry, essay, dialogue: poem, proposition, conversation: the infinity of desire, the specificity of argument, the fervor of speech . . . A work of poetics aspires to all three conditions, creative, analytical, and dialogical acts all aspects of a certain practice of language. This, then, is how I propose to define poetics.

Because of the intractable nature of the Palestinian/Israeli conflict in particular and the urgencies of the Mid-East crises in general, certain genre distinctions and modes of thinking and being can no longer be productively encouraged to persist. Such, in effect, is the argument of the writing contained in this book, conceived as a single unit in poetics.

In order to overcome an artificial border, we must overcome artificial borders in the way we think.

To bring down the wall, bring down the walls, in favor of the greater city. To build up public space, build up public space, honoring relationships between memorial art, funereal need, and commercial demand, as in the space that was called Ground Zero, and before that, The World Trade Center. Has any of this happened yet in one place, or the other?

Poem, essay, interview—*The New Babel* book brings together more than a decade worth of writing born from the double imperative I have felt as an American poet responding to both the Mid-East conflict and the problem of language . . . Language is the source of our humanity, and endlessly fluid, but it is also the source of a purposeful confusion that there is a necessity to counter, by way of new language.

The language of poetry is indeed various. In New York, in October and November of 2001, it seemed to me it had to be one, explicit way. Later, once the horrors of our wars in Afghanistan and Iraq had become patently obvious, it seemed to me it had to be written in another, more subtle way.

What comes to mind here is the conflict in the 1960s between the two great poets Robert Duncan and Denise Levertov. *The Letters of Robert Duncan and Denise Levertov* (Stanford University Press) charts the breakup of a friendship in poetry over the issue of the relationship of poetry to the Vietnam War. Denise Levertov argued for a straight-forward antiwar poetry, a *littérature engagée.*

For his part, Robert Duncan argued that the task of the poet is to imagine evil, not to oppose it, with the hint of a suggestion that in imagining evil we expose it all the more, especially in ourselves, rather than constructing an oppositional stance of us (good) and them (evil). This latter framework for good and evil, it goes without saying, would replicate the dominant paradigm of fundamentalist and neo-conservative rhetoric, and thus invalidate its own performance.

These two poets were friends, close readers of one another's work, individuals with the utmost respect for one another. They had been poetically aligned in the eyes of whatever literary world might have been attending to them from 1953 onwards. Yet their relationship was destroyed by their differing attitudes, and acrimonious exchange, concerning The War and its implications for Literature. That their relationship foundered on those rocks was largely owing to Duncan's own venomous injunctions against the turn Levertov's work took towards antiwar poetry and a vocabulary borrowed from the self-identified political left. Duncan may indeed have been the one responsible for the fall of the friendship, but for me he is also the one who was right about the larger point. For us then the question becomes how imagine maximally, which might mean enchantment as well as disenchantment, mystery as well as demystification, such that enchantment and mystery might also become interruptive of dominant modes of discourse . . . all the while still responding to a political and an ethical imperative?

Sometimes we are too quick to leap to the ethical, seizing the moral high ground for ourselves in the process. There are times when in a conversation it is smarter to seize the moral low ground as quickly as possible: one actually has to argue something in that circumstance, as opposed to asserting a tautological "it is good, therefore I am good." But what about circumstances like those of the Palestinians since 1948 . . . in which only an ethical vocabulary is available on the basis of which to make the case for a return, or for a just settlement? Then there are profound ethical and reflective resources that the Jewish prophetic and intellectual lineage makes available to us, and which may well have existed somewhere behind Denise Levertov's position on poetry and The War.

The essays in this book explore this zone. In many of the essays I look to major figures within European Jewish traditions of philosophizing and writing—Martin Buber, Gershom Scholem, Walter Benjamin, Paul Celan—for a guiding aesthetic and ethos. The great Zionist philosopher Martin Buber's position that Israel/Palestine needed to be a bi-national state, even to the point of an Arab majority, looms large in its prophetic stance. These authors are placed in juxtaposition with poets writing in Arabic—from the classical Arabic poet Ibn 'Arabi, to the celebrated Palestinian poet Mahmoud Darwish, to the intriguing contemporary poet, Somayo el-Sousi, writing in her home in Gaza City through it all. These essays parallel questions that the poems, springing from more opaque sources, were posing for me, the unconscious becoming the conscious and from there a relationship to reading and the world.

The interviews in the book—with Israeli poet Aharon Shabtai, American poet Amiri Baraka, and philosopher Michael Hardt—suggest for their part some of the fashions in which there is an Israeli self-critique, some of the modes by which we talk through the relationship between the ethical and the political, and some of the ways we as Americans position ourselves vis-a-vis the Mid-East crises. All of the interviews come out of a radio program I host and produce, entitled *Cross Cultural Poetics*, for which I call by phone poets, writers, philosophers, artists, and performers all over the world, and whose consequent dialogues suggest a kind of porosity of the world to itself, which I would like to think enacts some aspect of Buber's dialogical ideal of encounter. At the very least I would like to think they represent an alternative form of talk radio!

Finally, there are once again the poems, which attempt the hard work of the epistemological, of establishing the boundaries of what can be known, of reframing the real.

L'imagination au pouvoir.

PART I

The New Babel

The New Babel

0

Babel of course is the fall of a Tower, followed by a vast, manipulated confusion of words.

Babble is language's beginning, before it's a language, while it's still song.

As Babel is both a ground and a zero, Middle English *grund* and Arabic *zefir*, *cipher*, Gallicized *zero*—let's call it Ground Zero.

Babel is defiance of the demiurge and hubris of the heart, ziggurat aimed at suns yet unborn, inside the mouth the mouth as desire: man creates gods.

Where before stood the North and South Phallus now yawns a smoldering Cleft, smoke subject to variable breezes.

The smoke contains bodies; we breathe one another. Thus, Babel is Kabul. We breathe one another.

As Ares broods over all the world's capitals: fragments of furniture spun from seized cockpits, strangers blinking into craters of Mars.

Babel is Kabul: Babel's a Bible in a motel room dresser in Birmingham, Alabama: Babel's the Battery Park Esplanade and the people still waiting in the airport in Santo Domingo.

Babel: the most beautiful girl in all of Kashgar, black haired, black eyed, maybe 13 years old, in a gay red dress, gazing admiringly at the foreign lady chance brought to her alley, gently, tentatively, mouthing a single phrase in English, addressed to that lady: "How do you do?"

Babel is mettlesome, its scrotum melted some, our mad extravagant metropolis, not bashful, still seeking the heights.

Babel was Mesopotamia, its era's only superpower: redound of Gilgamesh, modern day Iraq.

Babel is Baghdad, Babel is Belgrade, Babel's our backyard, a World that incessantly trades names with itself.

Babble in three languages, babble in three thousand: put on a bib.

A baby babbled of lions eating books. And those lions ate books: Babel is books on the shelves of the Bibliothèque Queer.

No rabble in Babel: everyone's speech an equally valid muse. Thus: bomb them with butter.

Here is the blade with which Babel's abolished, here are the furrows where Babel begins, which no seed can boycott.

Babel rinses its parents in sorrow, Babel rewards its makers with slowworms, Babel is birth, rebuilding with cranes all sorts of crimes, the way life is a dagger, the way all wars begin with some bed's disaster.

Who shaved her cunt with Babel's box cutter: born from the rubble, "ba" is for father, "ma" is for mother, sacred baboons patrolling her precincts.

Babel is Buddha dispensing with words, Babel is mating, thunder, whale blubber and rain, Babel is blame, Babel is ax, Babel is Bush-ben-Laden and fame.

As tall facades crumble like rockface, so many unbound mountains, Captain FBI simply offers "My bad."

Babble of waves, babble of wharves, of merchants and stores, city proud of its iron and brains: babble is braggart, babble is pulpit, babble's a word on the tip of your tongue or the trouble stored in a bull's flaring nostrils.

I'm down with the Tower of Babel.

I can't even enjoy a blade of grass unless I know there's a subway handy or record store or some other sign that people do not totally regret life.

Is stumble, is stutter, is stone smooth as skin, towers swaying the way they sway in the wind, as a person is always his tongue's own half-witting puppet.

Is the baker whose pancakes are unscalable, whose loaves are uncanny and sprinkled with pain.

Is flesh covered with brine, is bitumen cracked with fever, wolves in the blood howling to the gibbous heart.

Babel is the beaten ballplayer who goes ballistic; Babel is an icicle in your mouth as melodious as a flute, as percussive in its dripping as drums.

Tower whose twisted tendrils resemble trellis and grapes, destruction demanded by the Dionysus of east meeting west, an unwillingness to consent to any loss of the self.

Babel is nothing but the celebration of words, talk armed with torches, dreams capsized by bigger dreams, the truth of each crater, the "bang bang" that wakes one from dream, the gap between "it's an accident" and "my god it's intentional," the B1 Bomber they're building and building, the backlash and the backlash to backlash and the backlash to backlash to backlash, O Barrio of Barriers, *our* republic of fear.

Enough elasticity to move with the wind, enough stiffness so that people can't know the building is moving: Babel is bubblegum stuck to your face.

Babel is presence, Babel is absence: nothing but the celebration of presence. *No mas* to sacred explosions, *no mas* to the occupation of land: sacred explosions, the occupation of land.

Babel is how a man howls as he leaps from the heights, where no other man can hear him; Babel is that moment of imagining one can fly, a brevity that lasts forever in Babel's unconscious.

Babel is a ray of sunlight crashing earthbound, a rivulet of rays crashing earthbound, a field mined with light.

The Tower of Babel: word up.

If architecture is frozen music, then these melted, smoking shards are its melodies, its incandescent burial grounds—Babel become what begs you to sing it.

1

> . . . *it is precisely in the heat of the war that those deep social convulsions take place that destroy old institutions and remold man, that, in other words, the seeds of peace germinate in the devastations of war. Man's intense longing for peace is never so strong as it is at a time of war. Hence, in no other social circumstance are there so many strong impulses intent on changing the conditions that produce war. Man learned to construct dams when he suffered from floods. Peace can be hammered out only at a time of war, then and only then.*
>
> —Wilhelm Reich, *The Mass Psychology of Fascism*

How many waves has the moon generated in the Persian Gulf since 1991?

How many waves have the moon and the Atlantic collaborated on since 1491-and-a-half?

What was the total number of breakers to have risen from the earth's seas before life ever began?

Can one figure the number of waves the Pacific has wept since Nagasaki and Hiroshima?

They hang flags the way horses wear blinders; they hang flags in great abundance. They want wars, without realizing it.

They signal war, some realizing it and some without realizing it; they wave flags the way matadors wave red.

Each suffering silently in the silence of his, her, or its own bed; two faucets dripping out of sync; three sinks, four sinks, five sinks, each with a dripping faucet; all the seas whipped and tossed by colossal winds.

The Tower of Babel: landlocked, an abandoned worksite farmers come to quarry.

The Tower of Babel: in the text it's preceded by a Flood.

Inside a New Mexican waterfall comes more than water, more than gravity, less than anything this moment's coarsening could ever put in words.

It's natural for water to fall. It's natural for water to fall from cliffs and it's natural for towers to melt when exposed to overwhelming heat. This applies equally to shacks. October 7, 2001.

Mud huts have their own way of falling, of being destructively transformed. October 8, 2001.

The death of peace happened long ago but went unmarked by any stone or number.

The wars come in waves.

Collateral damage is a literary term but the text's main force falls on the text's opponent.

Poetry: death without peace.

August 6, 1945: unending death.

Dying each death. Refusing to kill. October 11, 2001.

October 12, 2001: No, those are my tax dollars.

As even grief gives way to its own self-indulgence. Bush's address to the Nation, September 20, 2001.

The Nation wallows in its own grief, the Nation's mistakes are glorified, laureled, transformed into heroic moments, sacrificial acts: acts that would have been unnecessary if earlier mistakes had been avoided higher up, among the elites; and indeed it may be said those who died sacrificed themselves for the oil elites' sins. Fall, 2001.

Neither innocent, nor deserving of the force of those flames: no one deserves the force of those flames, no one is innocent.

Grief. Just grief. Unadorned by heroic gesture, deprived of that heroic consolation the bereaved are presumed to need. But do the bereaved really need to see their dead as heroic? Or do the bereaved need to see their dead loves as those cheated of their lives by a gratuitous dialectic of disproportionate extremes?

Some other kind of gesture: some other kind of mission: some other kind of interior life.

Not the fireman who brought his siren to the Times Square Peace Rally, drowning each speech, each speaker, in the blare of his profession: but the firemen and women digging in the mass grave they were the first to declare a sacred ground.

Inside a New Mexican waterfall comes more than water, more than gravity, more than fatal plunge, something subtly less than a monotheist could ever put in words.

The number of waves the Pacific has wept since Nagasaki and Hiroshima will never stop increasing.

It's natural for water to fall. It's natural to imagine the end of the world. In imagining the end of the world we protect our way of life.

In those days in which answers are offered as self-evident, hammer out a new Tower of Babel: not confusion but words as the impulse to transmute the silence of dumb agreement, no longer numb before a single divine authority or empire.

Let a new Tower of Babel touch the sky. Let a new Tower of Babel bend responsively to the moon. Ishtar, Inshallah, Quetzlcoatl. Babble babble babble.

2

Perhaps someday there will be a reckoning for this tiny village of 15 houses, all of them obliterated into splintered wood and dust by American bombs. United States military officials might explain why 55 people died here on

December 1st . . . But more likely, Madoo will not learn whether the bombs fell by mistake or on purpose, and the matter will be forgotten amid the larger consequences of war. It is left an anonymous hamlet with anonymous people buried in anonymous graves . . . America's own anti-Taliban allies were horrified, claiming the targeting had been mistaken and that hundreds of innocents had been killed. It was "like a crime against humanity," said Hajji Muhammad Zaman, a military commander in the region.

—Barry Bearak, The New York Times,
December 15th, 2001, Madoo, Afghanistan

Madoo's farmers are people in pieces. They've become their own fertilizer . . . assuming the rains come, we did them a favor, suggests a cartoon version of Secretary of Defense R. (Big laugh). But there isn't any need for such a cartoon. We've already firmly established the concept of collateral damage.

He who sees with his heart, as Paz would have it, sees Madoo as himself; and who can't see Madoo with his heart? ("Men with fossil minds, with oily tongues" suggests the cartoonist.)

Every face, a mask; every house a ruin of mud brick and wood.

Whose sisters were killed? Collateral Damage can't ever say beforehand. (Terrorists don't target specific sisters.) (The American attack came in four separate waves.)

After Madoo, to write poetry is barbaric (Theodor Adorno).

"'We've yet to find their bodies'"
"'many layers to this rubble'"
"'and now we live with this'"
"'mystery'":

Sayeth the elder Mr. Gul, Madoo resident,
though he might be speaking of Manhattan.

"Sorrowful old man" "white beard" "furrowed forehead":

"then Paia Gul" "young man" "bitter eyed": "'I blame'"
"'the Arabs'" "'then amended his own'" "'statement'"

"'I blame the Arabs'"   "'and the Americans'"
"'They are all terrible people'"
"'they are all the worst in the world'"
"'most of the dead were children.'"

Fragrance   bird song wheat fields
Mr. Bearak reporting two weeks after Madoo's apocalypse.
Harvesting scrap metal from bombs,
hopes of surviving winter.

Beyond anecdote sounds a hymn we can only hum, humble in our making,
the birds scribbling like authors in a startling ephemera of air.

"Walking in the vegetable patch
late at night, I was startled to find
the severed head of my
daughter lying on the ground.

"Her eyes were upturned, gazing at me, ecstatic-like . . .

"(From a distance it appeared
to be a stone, hallooed with light,
as if cast there by the Big Bang.)

"What on earth are you doing, I said,
you look ridiculous.

"Some boys buried me here,
she said sullenly."
—Araki Yasusada, *Doubled Flowering*, the foothills
surrounding Hiroshima, December 25, 1945

Craters. Tractor carcass. Dead sheep.
       Urn crushed to disc;
unendurable, "unintended," un-American
       Ax Americana;
far from Mecca, in Madoo, Tora Bora,
one undamaged room.

Anger cannot be buried.

Prayer is perfect when he who prays remembers not that he is praying.

Everything dead trembles (Kandinsky).

Note: E-Mail the reporter, ask if there were ever rows of poplars.

Moonstone sucked into the atmosphere of dwarfed arts; no Hero but also no Nero; the half that faces us is full tonight.

As the Kaushitaki Upanishad has it, "the breath of life is one."

The word "Madoo" is a transcription of a Pashto name the reporter must have sounded out.

In English, then, "Madoo."

In English the name "Madoo" derives from an old Scottish word meaning "my dove."

3

He imagined himself the famous wise man who'd succeeded in speaking with desert sand.

Not so wise of him to make the very sand in which he wandered quite so famed.

How wise was it for this well-dressed man surrounded by silence to continue to babble when no one was there?

There was plenty of air. All of it was very hot.

Twenty-one steps into the desert and the road disappears from view. Any sense of direction departs one's brain like a hummingbird. No one would know where you'd gone, nor would you.

The dunes are moving. The road disappears even if you remain motionless, planted in its middle. One might hire people to sweep the sand. But that takes money.

The silence of the Taklimakan is much renowned.

The Chinese built the road for oil trucks. To barrel through. And they do. Though it hardly matters. Trucks are little dots.

He imagined himself the obscure wise man who'd learned to speak with desert poplars.

"How do you live in a desert?" he asked an especially sturdy tree, and waited. For "truth" comes from "tree."

In a startling ephemera of air pinkness swirls from the goodbye sun, energy lifts from under its skirt, or perhaps it's the man, it's the man turning lavender with love.

And the desert poplar answered: "Put on a bib." Then added: "Please allow the word 'calm.'"

And the man went away, not sure he'd understood, not sure he'd ever spoken the tongue of desert poplars.

But he put on a bib. He wore the bib always. In the bedroom. In the boardroom.

When the other executives asked him what was happening he answered calmly: "I remain a kid."

The mind's future is never given.

Of course the wise man was eventually sacked.

The road had disappeared from beneath his legs.

Sand irritates the first sentinels.

My vocabulary did this to me, he thought.

I'll have to increase my vocabulary.

4

To begin to build the New Babel where the Old Babel had previously stood.

Babel is water freezing, despite the blinding sun, above a storefront grating on Broadway and 168th; Babel's an icicle that wants you to come over and stroke it through your warm leather glove.

To rebuild lower Manhattan, as Hiroshima was rebuilt, however comparatively small the scale of this new destruction, cormorants drying their wings in a warm stream of air.

"*Kom*, beside near, by with. Germanic *ga*, Old English *ge*, together. Latin *cum*, come with. Suffixed form *kom-tra*, in Latin *contra*, against, suffixed form *kom-yo*, in Greek *koinos*, common shared."

Thus: it's come time to come, it's past time to come against (patriotism as bobbled libido).

Babel is the only acceptable weapon, a tongue in your mouth, then someone else's tongue in your mouth; a tongue in the mouth is the only acceptable weapon and here comes someone else's tongue.

Babel is never, ever commodity; Babel is never ever ever commodity, since commodity fells it.

Liberate desire from commodity, though lingerie is desirable; Babel is contradiction without being hypocritical, commodity enticing care.

Babel is hands on shoulders, caresses for the breasts, uninterrupted burning apple wood, uninterrupted shining cherry wood, mists sprung from inner sinews and moistening lips.

How rhyme the whole of a redwood? That's the flower Babel has growing in its brain.

Babel's a belly as flat as a book, a curve as gentle as a dune, a dream as supple as a gymnast.

A cock edging into your mouth, vulva encircling your middle finger: babble's home.

Babel is the desire to affirm when you know it's not possible, a bulge in your pants as soft as the rock a petroglyph maker carves into; Babel's a nose unconventionally long that nonetheless turns you on, a twist in the argument that leaves you suddenly speechless, the Biblical prophets when they fall back in awe, tunnels of the cranium no spark has ever flown down before, learning not only to wield the great wheel but also to yield to it.

Babel's a snow leopard whose presence commands silence, a tiger you transform into the moment your lids are lowered, a dog with his nose up another dog's ass; Babel's a clean hyena and a dirty hyena, a clean hyena and a drooling hyena, a clean hyena and a meerkat with an awfully pointy head.

Babel's the bubble always bursting, the banks going bankrupt, the form of pleasure that costs you nothing but your own energy as you generate it.

Babel's a series of caresses that pass one into another.

Babel involves taking it upon yourself to stand, head bared, beneath the tempests of the Lord, in order to seize the Father's lightning with your hands, and offer the people this gift of Heaven, veiled in your song (Holderlin).

As I am ready to honor you and to blaspheme against you at one and the same time, my mind the mosque in which man and woman mingle—Mr. Last Monotheistic God Still Standing.

Babel is consciousness and comsciousness, cocksciousness and cuntsciousness, and comsciousness and consciousness taste here, and here, and here . . .

Working hypothesis #1: a precise for love and not precision bombing.

5

Nerves shrouded beneath the burka, as prescribed in certain countries; one's eye encountering only the burka, as experienced in certain cultures: whole realms in which men require one another to live behind the burka.

Not the techno-veil of consumer culture but the techno-burka, without any hole for the head.

It is a savage sensibility, savage and delicate, scored by superabundance and need, scandalized and desensitized by its own hunger for violence. Its adolescents shoot up their own schools, their own peers, then commit suicide. Their culture is a death mask, the burka its insignia, hooded hordes saturated in a thuglike, thinglike cult of senseless hurt, spawned by the most sophisticated marketeers.

The interior burka which impedes apperception, the heavy burka that goes with me, the opaque burka whose presence mocks reflection, the mandatory burka worn in the body politic, the bottled burka concealing the body from the erotic self, the bad opposition of burka and bikini, and other strange customs practiced there: to pretend power is not rooted in sexual urgency, to shift the burden of such urgency onto children unprepared to bare it.

Self-inflicted concealment always falls to self-reflection's raid, or so the Enlightenment taught and founding fathers bathed; "the eye that avoids seeing, sickens."

No Orientalism, no exoticism, no dehumanization of the other: our citizens refuse to any longer wear the black or turquoise burka.

No refuge in victimhood, in uniform amnesia, in hooded subjectivity: Americans will no longer throw a burlap sack over events that happen elsewhere in the world, will no longer squint at the world from behind their security burka.

No nationalism that blinds one to the terrible crimes of the Nation: the Attorney General will no longer throw the burka over the crimes he himself perpetrates, nor will the Secretary of Defense.

No false modesty, no passing on the buck: the Presidency and other machines of capital are no longer concealed by their various and sundry burkas.

Papers fluttering from the Tower of Babel's burning windows indicate that words are all that's left; paper survives where flesh and beams are shattered. Thus Babel is never burka and humans must honor bones with words.

Babel survives the revelation of its own mystery, as do women; the burka is nothing but its own formless bulk.

Burka is the triumph of the masculine over the feminine, banishing the feminine from public life, as words are banished from public life in a culture in which the reality of words are hidden.

Babel is the masculine that strives to reach the feminine and always fails, in falling back begins to live itself in all its seed potential.

Babel is the feminine ambition and potentiality of all things, inclusive of those specialized cells that strive for verticality.

If one could seize the dead stars and gather all those stones in one place in order to construct a tower . . .

And yet the body floats in a placenta of words and no word is ever comprehensible except as it emerges quivering from between the legs, naked as the space between the legs, and, in the next twinkle, comes howling, soon to fall back again, no more but no less than the words it has quickly scattered . . .

It's the little pin that pricks the giant balloon (Oppen). It's the sperm racing for the egg. A firing that has nothing to do with missiles.

Working hypothesis #2: a precise for love and not a precision bombing.

6

bobble	libido	brain	Pentagon	seclusion
village	Allah	songbirds	sisters	lavender
mystery	metal	Emir	American	icicle
children	daisy	plumes	mud brick	phallus
sheep	Quetzlcoatl	airport	Orphic	President
bib	life-fire	farmer	feminine	vegetable patch
moonstone	Mecca	Manhattan	Pashto	apperception
moonstone	Mother	poplar	dam	prayer
ax	E-Mail	hallooed	daughter	downtown
kiss	Oriental	precision	grief	Scottish.

7

What's worshipped isn't upstairs. You've kissed it often beside the sweet flanks of living oak, which is why you know it to be peripherally, pictured and unpictured thought, a wet rush between the legs, a bond between contingent realities and Babylon's tower, for which will yet come a fitting word.

The flowerpots break around you, the tortoise shells lose their markings, at that moment when the city seems to come unbound. Like the Cultural Revolution all over again, the Fathers sent to the countryside, the break with the Mother final, Central Park stretching outwards like a vast, slow-motion expanse, scattered with bystanders frozen in their disbelief. You knew your skin would forever hunger, that tears and their accompaniment would always sound out the absence of words; Big Character Posters would be the business of the day, that, and rousting dens of tigers. By December green water collects in the crater pit.

Yet "the deeper unsatisfied war beneath and behind the declared war" (Duncan), the conflicting egotisms, the hooligans of hubris, combat groups, policies of chaos, and petroleum spread, all yield to a larger dialectic. Abundances explode around you, the bounty hurtles past, and is even more wrenching for its beauty: boulders and blinding sun.

And the tongues were so baffled that each became scatterbrain to his friend, until not even the husband and the wife any longer knew how to speak with each other . . . murderers hard at work above ground, and all you have are these perceptions organized in little packets of dynamic resolve, memory and anticipation making reciprocal stands, having by now long since accepted the most difficult brain assignment our tribe can ever be charged with. Dazzling.

Sand irritates the first sentinels.

"Save those who weep" (Eluard).

What's worshipped isn't upstairs. Because this is already the uppermost floor. As Bina, in Bengali, refers to the instrument that Saraswati, goddess of learning, was destined to strum. Feel the tautness of those strings. Remember the books with torn covers and cover pages and thus no titles and authors: words read in their purest form, books acquired on the sly, *a fire finally acknowledged as impossible to put out.*

What's worshipped isn't upstairs. Because this is the ground floor. Among mysterious plants you bask in someone who's your sun yet rests beneath you, like a foundation. Run your fingers between her toes. Cracks of a source that holds marvel on marvel.

Things do assemble in their own rotunda; a wood stork hunches in the cypress, part of a greater ecosystem, without any particular capital or center.

The hour really is getting younger.

Winter 2002

PART II

Poems

Six Ways Two Places at Once

1

Collage is empty
and the gorge of the frogs

mighty deep,

everyone in that valley,
including the frogs,

as silent as yucca.

Tacit tanks target distant ocean's waves
human rights receding, crash of armored tide
now bobs, now bombs
news of the heavy wedding many dead
and child's brightly naked teeth.

And the wind in the oak leaves
as soundproofed
as the inside of a lobster.

The cueing machine tells of spring snow.
The cueing machine tells of spring snow
but I once rode an escalator which,
without warning, reversed directions.

The Pentagon rises like a phoenix,
even larger than before.

Groaning under an Administration
steeped in oil, lighting fires as it steeps.

"To keep the whole capacity
of the potential intellect

constantly actualized."
To keep the whole capacity
of the potential intellect
constantly actualized

and now, if your ears are nimble,
you can hear July 4th frogs
proposing to July 4th frogs
in the gully of July 5th.

2

The silence of perception
is the flesh of the book
opening itself
to the wondering reader.

And the name aids you
in its very impenetrability.
Nature fills the emptiness of the sign.

Music/mother tongue
a clarinet shines
like a sealskin.

Listen:
the life-world of the destroyer-nation
surly with commuter traffic,
its deepest consonances
muffled.

Look: a TV nailed to an oak tree
transfixes the worshippers in deafening.

Listen, look:
the polymorphously conceptual Father
a harbor seal barking philosophy from the piers
and the rocks.

Proteus is his name.
Proteus is also rich, dark coffee.

Have skimmed for a word of the first language
in a black bound Bible
and in the dismantled lightening
lining the heavily trafficked
super highways.

Road kill after road kill,
Proteus-bled.

The silence of perception
is the cry inside the flesh
surging towards
the letters of its exile.

3

Memory passes into formal knowledge; knowledge begets
capacity and power; power permits forgetfulness.

Such is the symmetry of the two-way bridge
between oppressor and oppressed.

Amongst all the atrocities
I shrug,
motoring in my new car
up the causeway, out past
Indulgence Farm—that robust enterprise—
far from the light of the little lighthouse
of First Anger.

Nix to logic,
nein to recognition,
nope to news
that stays news.

Nay too to the opposable human thumb?

Blood off the coastal waters:
the radio says you are better off
taking the bridge.

To wipe the footprints of toppled towers
off of curtainless cities
through whose windows
the moon stares:
to wipe the fingerprints off murdered continents.

Thus the Jenin atrocities were never documented.

I'll take the bridge
I'm taking the bridge right now
not to plunge into the morass
the private drama of guilt
is merely the scum over,
not the climax.

4

Taught to fear
complexity,—
to beware shifting
boundaries,
the self insists on boundaries
hard and fast.
Or so the moral community
proposes,
its posture headquartered in pious depression about
its own fate, its lack of reputation
in consumer society,
and most of all, its absence *of courage.*

Never assume there is one
who can speak clearly
into the contradictions
of non-identity and loss
or that such a person's

knowledge of suffering
extends to his organization, or to us.

Yet there *is* a victim under all the formulas,
surreptitiously subscribed to and conceded
by all to be a *necessary evil,*
denied any intellectual
status or *recognition* by all parties involved
because less valued.

What's worse,
men who out
of the desperation of their lives
try not to exist
by blowing up the dancers
with themselves?
Or a whole system
howling "Sub-Humans"
and acting on that precept,
having pursued in tanks
the tortured
right into their ruined hives?

I grow strong hearing myself
unable to justify it all,
falling silent . . .
false words only promote
the affliction.

Security forces preempt security
in favor of their own
regularly scheduled
programming.

5

Occupation again, and the tanks that bring occupation
arrive to padlock every dimension of everyone's life.

After the military incursions
ethical fires burn in every woodland
of A Country, in every city where the incursion is applauded,
urged, rationalized,
in every room where persons not in that room
have *their* existence denied.

1) After the burnt offerings and the black milk . . .
2) After the bulldozers and the bantustans . . .
3) Tears pour forth from nubile ground.
4) And the stars, full throated and welling.
5) A peacock broadcasts theology.
6) Violence will not be put to rest by violence.
7) Only after acts of creation can come a day of rest.
7) Violence will not be put to rest by violence.
7) There is no Sabbath during occupation.
7) And Occupation said
let there be light:

A leprous light entrenches itself during occupation.
No ambassador from these fingers to those,
not in this leprosy.
Theology infiltrates the very stones;
7) geology is theology is fence.

7) Marina Tsvateyva once wrote
"All poets are Palestinians."
While an Israeli who writes in Arabic—
an Arab Jew, he longs for Baghdad
before the expulsion—unfurls his latest text.

7) Helicopters empty their fire, tanks roll, writers write,
as Jenin takes place, echoing Shatila.
From the Negev to New York
my tribe is going mad.
In my distress I call upon a Lord
I don't believe in (7)
but the Jewish Arab
from Baghdad, writing in a language

his new land despises
dreams for seven nights
is **real**   . .

The very being of language
implies an other with whom to speak.
Language is always the other spoken to.
Each hill of Jerusalem knows that,
next year in
cry indeed unto.
next year in.

6

The city of New York once achieved fame
for its disclosure
of a previously unknown language
within a language
that yet remained mysterious.

Now sacred and profane wars
flush out all vanity
from the tall grass
of former meadows and woodlands.

Day and night an outpouring
of scare tactic warnings
trade on the gap between
words and awareness,
zones of ambiguous utterance
closed by the authorities
until further announcement.
Liberty Avenue and
the slave burial ground
form a single Main Street.
The new militarism annexes my sleep.
Sacred and profane conspire to justify
the one disconnect.

Sacred and profane
justify garrisons
in rainforests
and peach orchards.
The city beckons me into its logic
of mutually assured midnights.
Each siren announcing the last siren.
Each emergency an ember of all emergency.

Not that fire but another fire.
Not bomb by bomb obliterating
more merchandise
Empire then remaps
in its own image,
but instead witnessing
an image you'd never have guessed at
emerge from emergency.

Born of a love with no past
a city speaks within us
in unexpected journeys,
wine-dark dictionaries
foaming with words and opacities.

"Birthday of a new world"
Thomas Paine wrote in his proposal
for American revolution:

black copters crouched
in newfangled flowers.

Winter 2005

Invitation

the house cannot get in
the house cannot come in
the house cannot stay out
the house cannot get out
　　—Rodrigo Toscano

No symphony proves fruitful,
　　　　or Hebron.
Not theoretical considerations, not physical existence,
　　　　or Hebron.
To say "information" is not information
but an inkling of intensive form.
But do we, literally, unfathomable?
Say "Jenin," say "Nablus."
This will not be true of an inessential content
or Gaza.
And for each crutch sat seven without limbs.
　　　Or Tulkarm, or Ramallah.
In a mode
forgotten to man,
a million inmates.
Or Gaza.

All our tumult
tumbles into words,
turning them to windows of salt.
Of cells and sun
falling on the prison cells,
the sharpest rays illuminate
the longest jail blocks,
they will grow in the sunlight
of a special economy.
An original, profoundly superficial,
　　　or Jenin.

Scores of dead, send in
live doves. Each hoe held in the hand
of a hated rival. Beat their beaks.
Not grasp the birth pangs of a twig.
Say information, say to a woman
"Gaza, strip."
Occupied by one's own gaze,
seeing only what one wants to see.
          Or Bethlehem.

Yes.
Yes, your visa will expire at the end of this poem.
Yes, you will need a new passport to exit
this nightmare, a new genre of passport.
If every veteran of reality rose up and protested
every single case of war mongering . . .
          or Jenin.
In the prison yard convenes a court
for shooting hoops. Shooting hopes,
all who enter here.
          Or Hebron.
Unlike the words of the original text
orthodox *experiences* remain fire-proof:
just give me the rock.
Pass me the damn Dome of the Rock
or rebound it, rebind it, ban travel both ways,
          or Bethlehem.
Dribbled away in a mode
forgotten to free men,
which the Committee against Torture
finds to constitute torture.
Never to liberate the language
imprisoned in the rock.

The Tomb of the Patriarchs, forever and ever.
Oh, he was wed to his wines, cheap as chickens.
And of course he was strung out,
which is his God Given Right.
          Or Qalqiliya.

Slapped buttocks
in explicit jeans
no one dares talk about.
                    Or Tulkarm.
Didn't the river need seven dams to block its waves?
A freshly pierced goat's heart,
flung into the tracks tank treads leave
in mingled bloods and mud.
These lands of little men.
In their white frothy bliss,
their ability not to see,
steak for me and steel for you,
doctors without borders for all those devils
inconveniently jostled,
kept by curfew from even their cemeteries.
But the cemetery is our library,
our archive, our garden!
This is not true of an inessential content,
                    or Gaza.
This is forever, for forever and ever.
                    Or Nablus.

This is forever, for forever and ever.
Trauma irrigates new channels of hate.
                    Or "Hebron":
a decisive detail evolving only in language,
a flux substantiating the published,
or Gaza.
                    Beit Rama, Salfit, Artas,
a liquid spectacle of "facts on the ground,"
forced to strip and march at gunpoint.
                    Or Ramallah.
Unable to grow a single blade of grass
without the Others permission.
Did I mention the moon
reflected in the silent waters
of the Dead Sea?
That you thought you had done with crossing
sad tracts of land, those that made of you and your travails

amazing additions to the constant stone you wearied?
      Or Jericho.

Dearest Father
(important listener)
ask that ancient washerwoman
if there is anything left to wash,
anything left to grow.
      Or Ramallah.
Dearest Rumi says that if you are unthankful for the fruit
all the other forms turn ugly too.
      Or Hebron.
The belt that is the waist about to heal.
Dearest olive groves confiscated by the courts.
The waist that will not heal, freshly belted.
Never felt living beings within you?
Visit this cemetery,
dig into these roots of light,
lose yourself in earth.
Silence capsizes into a glass kingdom,
vast and perceptual, shattering
all your links to the former caravan.

Dearest Mother.
      Or Hebron.
Sand the color of shattered stone,
in which sits a big part of my past.
Dearest Mother,
calling Gaza.
Dearest Mother, dearest Father.
Land that sobs from its own contractions,
never rid of itself, syntax beyond aching,
never actually giving birth.
Quivering in the wheat field
from so much female,
too many mounds of remembrance,
too much musk and haunch.
And the sun clasps all of it,
blood-stained and precious,

to its sensors.
Calling Gaza.
Culling Gaza.
Calling Gaza.
        Or Hebron.
To say "information" is not information
but an inkling of intensive form.
Of necessity therefore the demand
for literalness.
Gaza.
        Or Hebron.

Occupational Hazards

Palestinian Transfer

Of olive groves spread out across soft hills the people despair: *everything here has been marked, and everything marked is lost.*

Transfer isn't necessarily a dramatic event.

The telephone just keeps ringing and ringing. Something like a stethoscope against the breast. Clinical.

In this way three children break an afternoon curfew and are mortally wounded.

The current situation calls for a swift and speedy effort to control all forces: not only as freedom struggling with its conqueror, refusing its reification and its perverted image, but as the being of groves spread across the hills, raising their fruits like tiny fists, by some unimaginable patience holding back the punch that would provoke the conqueror further.

The ruined, arid land, the neglected trees, testify that promises nourished from afar didn't create an organism strong enough to withstand the assorted—well, you know all that already. Like a stethoscope against the chest.

To show how and why a non-violent person, like myself, becomes violent. Not that I have become violent.

Uneasy rapprochement, for the sake of others. That explains the contradictory character certain states of mind are charged with, a clap of thunder when no storm is visible.

As for the psychosocial trance I would like to say one last thing about Steven Biko.

Festering wounds ask questions of their father. Like a refrigerator that groans from its own inner cold. The telephone just keeps ringing and ringing.

The 36

It was while the army demolished a neighboring house, belonging to the family of a militant from Islamic Jihad, that the wall fell on the Makadmah family.

Opposition came swiftly from the 36 hidden justices.

There they are, you will have to go a long way around if you want to avoid them.

I would like to stroll within range of your rifle. I'm that angry.

Then an explosion, and the wall fell on the assembled family.

The name might be derived from a root meaning "to come" or "be present": or possibly from another one meaning "to bruise."

The last child the father and his neighbors found, scratched but alive.

Beauty is enhanced by this single moment of peace, and his hand, which clutches the rubber ball, and Being never at any time running its course with cause and effect coherence.

That our predicates do not contain untruths but are simply claims gone unfulfilled in our contemporaries and in us. Being-in-the-thick-of-it.

When the building came down I felt a disconnect, a complete loss of apperception, as well as a completely leveled perception of things.

Mountains of night creep away without ever again yielding to barest day.

With ambulances blocked from reaching the scene, Mrs. Makadmah, 41, died while neighbors were carrying her to a clinic.

Her name might be derived from a root meaning "to come" or "be present," or possibly from another one meaning, "to bruise."

Expect no trial.

Except in every single action we are engaged in.

Possibly mixed among our neighbors, the 36, hidden and just.

Concentrated within themselves they go unrecognized by their fellow men.

Mrs. Makadmah was known as an excellent cook who often made cakes and cookies for her children.

The Israeli Army expressed regret.

Click Here to Receive 50% Off Home Delivery of The New York Times.

Essential Services

Essential services in several critical areas, including health, education, water, electricity and law enforcement could no longer be provided.

What good would running to the Occupied Territories have done, what good running away?

The bridge, much like the airport, the border crossing or any other entry point, is a place of enduring humiliations—homologue to the denial of history.

The fiancée arrived, surrounded by her brothers and sisters, all seven of them.

This quarter 17 killings were carried out that were almost certainly assassinations.

My grandmother and grandfather go to the rail of the boardwalk and look down at the beach.

If you throw even a cursory glance at the past you will observe that in the continuum of colonial control apartheid and peace have never been coextensive.

After his village was razed the Leper approached the soldier cradling his Uzi.

The ocean is becoming rough; my grandmother observes that the waves come slowly, drawing their strength from far back.

With pious and gentle resignation the persecuted ones suffered such intolerance (though later, in the Warsaw Ghetto . . .).

If the Law is texture, that texture must have changed. Been smoothed out by its "triumphs."

To cope with interruptions and delays all schools in the West Bank begin to make up classes, when possible, during off days and holidays, as if by the sheer quantity of hours the circumstance could be overwhelmed.

The power of redemption seems to be built into the clockwork of life.

Out of stasis and paralysis, symptomatic of ghettos in general, I decided to run there and not to run there.

A stone   roars   like   a   bird   Slaughtered
Tahseen Alkhateeb writes from Amman.

Not genocide, not ethnic cleansing: a name has yet to be conceived for what is undergone in these curfewed quarters.

Certainly not "The Question of Settlements."

The Argentines speak of "The Disappeared" but that isn't it either.

Redemption and its blasted clockwork.

Penelope

She set up a great loom in the main hall, started to weave a fabric with a very fine thread. And every night, when the wooers had fallen asleep, she would unthread that day's work.

Penelope transfers her strength to the medium of her subjective expression, in order to then subordinate herself to that medium, more than subjective, in the act of destructive defiance.

On the other side: only eight outposts established since 1996 have been completely dismantled. Many see this expansion as positive.

Weaving done in oneself insures that one won't spill a drop of another. Then one undoes one's own weaving. This is not just a ruse.

The awesome power of sacrifice. I tracked its meaning, never examining the sources of power that allowed me to make my own tracks, and thus, erasing them in the process.

Every day I would weave my father-in-law's shroud, and every night by torchlight I would unweave that same web.

At least let her finish her weaving before you possess her. No. The bulldozer kept coming.

I'm no expert but I think I see a problem here.

If Palestine is Penelope, Penelope has already waited more than 54 years.

Odysseus

Other tales there are to tell, almost as sad, said Odysseus.

Words gather inside those exiled from space, those receding into time. Treat the person in whom they gather as if that person were their own sick child. Like parents made magically young in the tending.

You seek a homecoming as sweet as honey, since once every soul and soul-root had its special place in the *pleroma*. All instantiations of the return prove false. All fixed images of home prove idol.

Yet contagious as laughter or yawning there remains an unfathomable quality that frees language from something like description. Which remains undescribed, tantalizing.

Every day I would weave at the great loom; every night I would tear my work to shreds.

My guiding light, said Penelope, is the Israelites: they waited two millennia.

Under the name Reb Areb the poet Jabès offers. "Jewish solidarity is the impossible passion one stranger can feel for another."

Penelope, calm and straightforward: "death will surely come to the suitors."

He stripped off his rags and revealed himself as who he really was: a seed in the celestial granary, the perfect tension between particularism and universality, the voluptuous pleasure of silence fusing with anger.

Penelope one's waiting, Odysseus one's wandering.

Odysseus always no more than Penelope at her loom, weaving the future.

He her thought, she thinks, in one guise or another, for more than two millennia.

Transcendental Tabby

An Introduction to the "Apple Anyone" Poems

To say that the transcendental is historically constituted amounts to saying that universality cannot be assigned to it; it is necessary to think of a particular transcendental. But after all, there is nothing more mysterious than what is collectively called a culture.

—Guy Lardeau, "L'histoire comme nuit de Walpurgis"

In such manner Guy Lardeau invites us to contemplate a contradiction—the particular transcendental. Contradiction, because one of the attributes of the transcendental is held to be its universal grounds. Contemplation, because that is what the mind does, at least one committed to both a cognitive process and a mode of thought that goes beyond the simply analytical. One concept that may occur to us here is "strategic transcendentalism": one holds a condition to be transcendental or necessary to perception itself for specific political or tactical purposes. Another phenomenon that may come to mind here is that of the lyric poem: the lyric poem is a construct capable of maintaining equilibrium among contradictions and as such is singly able to accommodate the needs of such a slippery imperative ("negative capability"). Surely the allure of the poem is partly this, and the concomitant promise of mystery without belief. Our texts are the living evidence of an ethics of ambiguity.

I positioned the transcendental lyric in like manner in my essay from the 1990s "A Flicker at the Edge of Things." Things here—"here" variously meaning in what passes for my mind, the room in which I sit and write, America, the shifting continents—flicker, and poetry is still the flicker at the edge. Some edges are as eternal as the need for a center, others are as ephemeral as perspective. What the language needs at any given moment shifts. The more things change, the more things change. You can never put your river into the same flume twice, because that would already be water under the bridge, and so on and so forth. The transcendental signifier, floating downstream, over flumes and under bridges, is like the spindle or seed of some plant, waiting to be thrown to the bank by a particularly violent movement of the water, where it might take root. A fluid foundationalism is always sensitive.

Now the particularly violent movement that has provoked a necessary literary response in its aftermath is the Western recoil against the Arab and Islamic worlds. "Orientalism," so utterly exploited by European colonial powers and so carefully dissected and exposed by the late Edward Said, found a new bloom of its own in the Bush Administration's version of what we are at war against in the Islamic world. Paid pundits speak of a "clash of civilizations." The White Man's burden, which was to civilize the native, is reconstituted as the necessity to bring democracy to those in the Middle East yet too primitive to know this sacred form of government. We know all too well what violence has been unleashed in our names on the basis of these and other related ideological precepts. At the edge of things we watch with horror, demonstrate with desperation, and write vociferously. In 2001 Andrew Joron wrote in his "The Emergency of Poetry: "What good is poetry at a time like this? It feels right to ask this question, and at the same time to resist the range of predictable answers, such as: Poetry is useless, therein rests its freedom. Or, poetry has the power to expose ideology; gives a voice to that which has been denied a voice; serves as a call to action; consoles and counsels; keeps the spirit alive." For Joron, none of these functions suffice. There is only one function that is efficacious. That is the lament. "The lament, no less than anger, refuses to accept the fact of suffering. But while anger must possess the stimulus of a proximate cause—or else it eventually fades away—the lament has a universal cause, and rises undiminished through millennia of cultural mediation. Unlike anger, the lament survives translation into silence, into ruins."

For me Joron's lament is resonant, at least of one phase of our writing under the current imperative. The other phase has involved a working with language that might undermine the nauseating dichotomies that underpin the justification of Empire, the clash of civilizations, and the erosion of civil liberties. Poetry is language, and in poetry false dichotomies can best be dissolved, since the false dichotomies themselves are only frozen language.

Thus I set out to write a series of poems using only English words derived from Arabic. Later that seemed a further segregation, and I collaged those materials with Shakespeare cut ups and rewrites—the name "Shakespeare" conjuring up the conservative pride and core of "English"—and I kept doing this until I had the "Apple Anyone Sonnets."

Languages are interdependent, as are cultures. The texture of one can be raised up and felt in another. Some of the words I used later were discovered to be of Persian origin, or of contested origin. (As for example the word "mulatto": of course the word "mulatto" would be of contested origin.) That isn't the point. The point is the one Lardeau makes: there is nothing more mysterious than what is collectively called a culture. Robert Duncan's observation (since confirmed by many medieval scholars) that the figure of Beatrice in Dante's *Divine Comedy*, presumably the very pinnacle of Christian literary art, is in fact drawn from Islamic Sufi sources, might also be offered as a particular material evidence of the strangely synthetic nature of all culture. Or else Ron Silliman, who writes: "the words are never our own. Rather, they are our own usages of a determinate coding passed down to us like all other products of civilization, organized into a single, capitalist, world economy. Questions of national language and those of genre parallel one another in that they primarily reflect positionality within the total, historical, social fact."

If it is a privilege to be able to allow one's brain to travel in thousands of directions all at once (and it is), then part of the responsibility of that privilege remains the imagination of positionality in relation to a proposed total grid, just as Silliman argues. Of course this move is dangerous, because it bears a structural resemblance to the imagination of Empire, in which all points are united or yoked into a single system, around a center. This danger is only heightened by the circumstance that "English" is the imperial language. Yet there is no backing away. Consider, then, the direction Kamau Brathwaite takes when exploring the possibilities of Caribbean poetry: "Nation language is the language that is influenced very strongly by the African model, the African aspect of our New World/Caribbean heritage. English it may be in terms of its lexicon, but it is not English in terms of its syntax. And English it certainly is not in terms of its rhythm and timbre, its own sound explosions. In its contours, it is not English, even though the words, as you hear them, would be English to a greater or lesser degree." ("History of the Voice.")

Thus the work remains a question of defamiliarizing language as a natural condition, of allowing poetry, a language within a language, to open like a sluice, of changing the language from the inside, of being aware of the silence within words that allows for such liberating motion, of arriving at a new language by way of an exploration of the old. That is to say, *American* is a post-colonial language too. Individual consciousness liberates itself from the colonies English establishes within it by burning a new language within those very social cities so established by history. If the idea of the transcendental, which implies a detachment from the immediacy of the social, and the idea of the lyric, which implies an ecstatic upswell, still speak to us, it is because they allow us not a greater social mobility (obviously not!) but a mobility in the preconditions which make what is to follow possible—some kind of society.

Let us resolve to think of transcendental mobility—as a mobile. The poem as a mobile of words and signs, dangled over the crib of the culture, as to stimulate the mind to imagine new combinations. Patriarchal poetry? Perhaps. Matriarchal intentionality? No doubt. Childhood, that deep alembic, crawls to maturity in floods of light. Names of fruit nourish unusual bits of unconscious truth. *Attabi* was a neighborhood in Baghdad where a certain kind of patterned tapestry was made. The word that named that neighborhood traveled to English as "tabby," which became a kind of cat that bore a similar pattern in its fur. A tabby has wandered into the room just now. It is the ghost of my former pet. It stares at me blankly, its black nose still black, its expression as empty as when it was alive. That gaze is without meaning until I begin to write. Quite suddenly a real being is gazing back, not a ghost, not a cat either, but a being that overflows its name. Not Jabes, not Celan, not Weil, not Darwish. Not Dante or Ibn 'Arabi. But not uninformed by those names either. Amidst the bounty of mid-summer a pair of eyes fill with signature and lament: broken, silent, resolute, voiced. At the fading ruins, they anticipate suns. Sediment is splendid. The dead and our living gaze are locked in love—and make for a third. The words are never just our own.

Apple Anyone 1

Shall I portray you as a blazing afternoon?
The freaking almanac didn't forecast amber rain.
Wind whipped to shreds ballyhooed Doppler readings
as your typhoon tongue lashed my latest wants.
So the sun's golden boasts are bested by bullying clouds,
each of our arsenals costing us our alchemy.
Yet no cloud shall dim my love's manic barbs.
Neither will my eyes become gauze, or ghouls;
no Nothingness shall brag of drowning me in Styx.
A single whiff from the carafe of years suggests there is more
to speech, a crocus thrusts at the barbarian of description
as long as it's a carob for a carob, a Copt for a Copt, Bedouins
lead us far into an arch-alcohol we're the ones to ferment.

almanac   typhoon   arsenal   alchemy   gauze   ghoul   carafe
crocus   barbarian   carob   Copt   Bedouin   alcohol

Apple Anyone 2

You are more orange than oranges, more red than blood orange.
Coffee masks enervation, I'm still awake, checkmated by night;
life packs in too much racket to know calm's truest state and form.
And during the day its way too hot, thanks to the pushy sun.
Thus the safari is unshackled from its safety net.
So rice is checked, guitars jar, spinach is lacquered in a can.
In the constant flux of things all good from goods must fail.
But you do not mask from sight those gifts you possess,
alchemy on a wavy mattress among lightly waving fronds.
In words to you groves will always glow, the purpose
of so many night presences suddenly made lilac.
So long as poets pick fruit, these hands pick you.

Orange   coffee   checkmate   safari   rice   guitar   jar
spinach   lacquer   mask   alchemy   mattress   lilac

Apple Anyone 3

As big waves flip out onto rocky coast so our days finish abruptly.
The ocean's tributaries show their dhows: appearance is a cipher.
As childhood, that deep alembic, in floods of light
crawls to maturity, where which to crouch, calling itself a King.
And as we change positions with what was finishing at our birth
hope builds its harem in serif, like rice collecting saffron.
A guitar-shaped bench trembles to its own rhythm!
Light wants to fix in place the flourish it dabs on things—
this great esplanade of sesame, magazines wide,
something wished for, made of marabout and lime.
As names of fruit nourish unusual bits of unconscious truth.
Nothing is born but for the sword to assassinate
and still, in their hiddenness, from red shift to red shift
I praise your alcoves, and the oceans wildest dilations.

dhow   cipher   alembic   harem   serif   saffron   guitar
sesame   magazine   marabout   lime   assassinate   alcove

Apple Anyone 4

I'm not going to dignify the proposition
that this our hazardous union of minds
has flaws—a kiss is not a kiss
which scuffs if it finds some scuffing.
I'm talking about a tattoo in thought,
something that can't be erased by monsoon's anger.
When you garb yourself for love, think sequined sash,
damasked but garbled minaret:
something that will appear a star for all those sailors
of unknown worth, like us, fleeing the latest massacre.
Constancy is no clock's fool; like kohl to lid
ear clings to lip until the drop-off point of doom.
If you can cinch it that I'm wrong, I'll shut up,
drop all my claims concerning the human carat.

hazard   tattoo   monsoon   garb   sash
damask   minaret   massacre   kohl   carat

Apple Anyone 5

Why is it my words always touch this particular?
I stay afloat on language I've plucked from Sufi summer,
my trysts with words the same one wooed, mascaraed, talced.
Though the lute of a genie is as outdated as last year's atlas,
though a belated troubadour sings of checkmate move by move,
yet no monumental rock shall outlast these our silly constructs:
that which glints brightly in such tariffed compositions
is a gazelle among orange groves, a mecca in the mouth.
Here comes a tabby whose scratch will leave a lasting mark,
or else a taffeta from a quarter of town recently hit by bombs,
or all the cotton ever picked, the laborious wizard enslaved inside you.
Why is it my words always touch this one particular?
As the sun is daily both bouncy and flat so we transact
only what we can minaret, darting among damasked ruins.

Sufi mascara   talc   genii   atlas   troubadour   checkmate
tariff   gazelle   orange   mecca   tabby   taffeta
cotton   wizard   minaret   damask

Apple Anyone 6

To go on in an ideology that is patrolled by admirals
all praised to the hilt, each awarded triple scoops of sherbet,
sugars gushing in banana and lime, or to grab up pails against
a whole Mediterranean of pain, and by opposing, drain it?
The road to Baghdad: it is an orgasm religiously sought.
To slow my brain and by night to say we stopped all that:
a saffroned vulture scuffs the dirt it lands in until every man
looks inward, acknowledging his own mulatto ground
and the thousand gauzy masks our bodies are mom to.
To slow my brain—to slow my brain!
And during that slowing to succumb to a new fantasy,
a woman with corneas like coffee beans, a coiled mortality
uncoiling, amalgam, not amalgam, that is not a jackal—
a vocabulary, a calamity, and at last, a casualty list.

admiral   sherbet   sugar   banana   lime   Baghdad
saffron   mulatto   gauze   cornea   coffee   amalgam

Apple Anyone 7

I lost contact with you for just one morning and all the music
turned to arsenic, in my mind I barely maintained your image.
Now, while you dream of ponies, petals gush from your eyes:
apricot o'clock, orange o'clock, after which comes lime.
So I am partly blind and partly sighted, like those blue shrubs
reputed to be filled with elixir of bird when all they really do
is interlock with whatever happens to pass, in pure contingency,
and its mostly birds, and grains of sugar, and amulet candy.
Over these shifting truths the mind has no hold, our hands
liming mascara into the tabbied skin of twilight, talismanic hour.
Mountain top and salt spray gush, all part of your massage.
Don't be naïve: they can send assassins by guitar too.
Yet quietude fills the carafe of hours, orange fills that quietude,
there is nothing yet to mourn: you are here, it is all still here.

guitar   arsenic   apricot   orange   lime   shrub   elixir   sugar
amulet   candy   mascara   tabby   talisman   gush   massage

Zero Hour

Last night a bit of moon appeared above this candle.
Coffee fell hotly into cups, so many footsteps of walking dream.
I sensed certain life forms, normally shy, strain against
their ghoul-freaked masks, seek the burning candle.
Then there was only the burning candle, nothing sought.
A single column of smoke rising beautifully and in error
as if beyond all amber, a single throat swaying
like some delicate giraffe's aloft over massaged savannah.
Alcohol sparkled on the way from the carafe;
on the sequined sofa of night I distinctly tasted scallion.
I beheld the first apricot of our being and a compass,
musky algebra and a throne of smoke thrumming grievously
in an ancient alcove, beyond mortal argument.
"I" is anchorless but authentic.
"I" is wax wetting the crimson amulet it is held in.
"I" is a vocabulary, a calamity, and again, a casualty list.

crimson   coffee   ghoul   amber   giraffe
massage   savannah   alcohol   carafe   sequin   sofa
scallion   apricot   algebra   alcove   amulet

PART III

Proposition and Interview

Interview with Aharon Shabtai

Aharon Shabtai is a leading Israeli poet and activist. His wife was the late Tanya Reinhart.

Leonard Schwartz: Welcome, Aharon Shabtai.

Aharon Shabtai: Good evening.

LS: You've had a new book come out in English translation entitled *J'Accuse*, translated from the Hebrew by Peter Cole and published by New Directions. Can you tell us a little about the work in this book?

AS: Yes. In Israel this collection is a part of other books, but here, in the English edition, there are only political poems. These political poems are usually written ad hoc and published ad hoc in *Haaretz,* the Israeli daily, which is more or less parallel to the *New York Times*. They publish a literary supplement every Friday. Sometimes I write something, and they are ready to publish it after two or three days. Sometimes they think that it's too much, and they don't allow it to be published. But usually I publish the poems. In the English edition, I collected only the poems that are relevant to the last years, to the tragic situation here. It's a political book.

LS: Yes, *J'Accuse* as a title obviously references Emile Zola's book . . .

AS: The poem "J'Accuse," for instance, they didn't want to publish it. I wrote it one week or so after it all began. They didn't want it. It took maybe a month until I found a smaller newspaper to publish it.

LS: A double-edged sword. You compare *Haaretz* to **the** *New York Times*—the *New York Times* never publishes serious or political or even engaging poetry of any sort. It's wonderful that *Haaretz* does that. On the other hand I can see that they have limits.

AS: They have limits, because they get a lot of letters from subscribers saying that they will not continue reading the newspaper. They get scared from time to time. And then they publish me again, because after all they also like to publish me.

LS: Let's go to the poetry for a bit. There's a poem in *J'Accuse* entitled, in English, "My Heart." I wondered if you could read it for us in Hebrew and then in Peter Cole's translation.

AS: Yes, but maybe I will tell you something about the poem before I read it. This poem was written two years ago, when, on Passover, the cities in the West Bank were conquered and there was the Jenin massacre. It began also in Ramallah, when the Israeli army entered there. I wrote it immediately. After I published this poem, I could not publish for some time, because afterwards they published, for three weeks I think, letters, very angry letters by the readers.

MY HEART

My lips mutter: Palestine! Do not die on me!
My heart's with each syringe in your hand, Moustafa Barghouti!

It's with the Muqata'a, with the roadside corpse that help couldn't reach—
with the pencil on your table, Mahmoud Darwish.

With the empty oxygen tanks at the clinic in Nablus.
Maha Abu Shareef, the soldiers who stormed into your house

pissed on the walls of my heart as well.
And now, for the wheels of a Red Crescent ambulance, that heart has become a footstool,

and for you too, Manaal Sufyaan, at Ayn Masbach,
lying in a pool of blood, shot by thugs on your porch.

Our country, a new birth is underway in Bethlehem—
the bloody placenta will be tossed into a pail, and from the womb

a creature born of our people's love will burst forth into the blue.
Listen, his heart is beating through mine—I'm a Palestinian Jew.

LS: Thank you so much, Aharon, for that poem. Could you say a little more about the impetus behind it, the way in which the Jenin massacre—but also the general assault on the Palestinians—has affected you as a writer and what you're doing in your writing in reaction?

AS: Basically, these people who are now persecuted are like the blacks or the Indians in America, or the Irish, or anybody. They are the people of this land. They are what is called in Greek the *autochthones*. They lived here before us, and they gave this land the beauty of the villages. And now they are put into ghettoes, their land confiscated. Think about New York—from Manhattan they are going to bomb Harlem. This is what it's like for me. Here we live in Israel-Palestine, these two peoples. It is something integral. If they are going to be expelled from here, I will also be expelled. For me, they are completely like brothers here in the land. This poem came out in the beginning. In the beginning, it was only occupation. Then the occupation settled into apartheid. Separate ways for settlers and for Arabs, confiscating most of the land and pushing them closer to the ghetto. Gaza is like a prison or concentration camp.

But now, since I wrote this poem, comes a new phase—the phase of ethnic cleansing. On a daily basis, all the laws of Geneva, and all the human and moral laws are broken. People get killed and houses are ruined. It is a slow and very subtle ethnic cleansing. Of course they cannot come to bomb and kill many people on one day, but in a piecemeal way, every day, when ten or seven or twenty are killed. Thousands are wounded, and they cannot get medical care because there are closures and they cannot move from place to place. So many people are dying like this. Trees are uprooted. I don't want to go on describing it, but it's something so traumatic, because these people are living near us, and we used to go to their restaurants, and we know them and they speak our language also, because we live together. It is something unbelievable that happens here.

LS: Even from the distance of this phone line, of America, the reality seems to be that the Palestinians have become the Jews, that the Palestinians are the Jews of the second half of the twentieth century and the beginning of the twenty-first.

AS: Exactly, I feel that because I was so much educated in and well read about the Holocaust. So I feel as a Jew and I try to help them because the Jews, our experience of thousands of years is the craving for justice, for human rights, for human solidarity. This is the ethos of our writings. And now suddenly here in Israel . . . it's such a change. We have now a completely militaristic society. There is, of course, still a layer of parliamentary life, but in fact this country is now run by the army and all the ministers, most of them generals. Everything is now decided by the community of the army and intelligence, and also by some rich people who go through them. It's a completely new Israel, what we see now.

LS: You've written very tellingly in other poems about the privatization that's taken place in Israel under Netanyahu and the loss of the socialist kibbutznik background in Israeli culture. But you're also suggesting that there's a way in which Sharon's policies are hollowing out the very basis of Jewish ethos, built up in act and thought over a very long period of time. So it seems that it's a crisis of Jewish consciousness as well as a more powerful crisis of Palestinian life and limb.

AS: On the one hand, it's a crisis for the Palestinians who live here now. This fence, this wall, is something terrible. And we are very active, we go there, to the wall, because it's not very far from Tel Aviv. We go to it and we try to help. But recently they have begun to shoot Jews who are protesting against the wall. This wall is going to confiscate most of the land of the villages there. The aim is to push them to run and leave their land because they cannot live without their land. It's also a crisis for us as Jews because, as I've told you, we live now . . . it's completely unethical . . . it's completely . . . unbelievable what happens here . . .

LS: It does defy language, doesn't it . . .

AS: I can't find the words now, I'm sorry.

LS: I understand. It does defy the ability to speak to it. Let's talk about . . .

AS: Such cruelty, such evil! And it's a country that doesn't know any law or any border. Israel has no borders at all like other countries in the world, and also no laws at all. It doesn't know anything concerning the laws of war, the laws of property. Everything is done ad hoc by this bunch of thugs.

LS: Aharon, I wondered if you could read to us again from the book, *J'Accuse*. There's a poem entitled "Passover 2002," which I think is very sharp and very powerful in terms of these questions.

AS: Yes, yes.

PASSOVER 2002

Instead of scalding
your pots and plates,
take steel wool
to your hearts:
You read the Haggadah
like swine, which
if put before a table
would forage about in the bowl
for parsley and dumplings.
Passover, however,
is stronger than you are.
Go outside and see:
the slaves are rising up,
a brave soul

is burying its oppressor
beneath the sand.
Here is your cruel,
stupid Pharaoh,
dispatching his troops
with their chariots of war,
and here is the Sea of Freedom,
which swallows them.

LS: You write, "You read the Haggadah/ like swine, which/ if put before a table/ would forage about in the bowl/ for parsley and dumplings./ Passover, however,/ is stronger than you are." Could you comment on those two lines?

AS: It's obvious, you know, Passover is the holiday of liberty, of liberating the slaves. And here, how can they sit two weeks from now and read the Haggadah when the people here, the Palestinians, the people of this land (I don't speak now about the hundreds of thousands of workers that come from all over the world and live here like slaves, but I speak of the Palestinians) live now in concentration camps. And I say this not without thinking, these are really concentration camps. Not death camps, but concentration camps. There is barbed wire and soldiers guarding them, not letting them go to their fields. These people are like the Jews in Egypt. They sit on their land, and they are slaves, they are prisoners in their own land. And these people, we know them, it's not people you can talk about in Chechnya or Afghanistan, these are people that we know very well. We eat in their restaurants, we know that they really want to live with us in peace, and they are enslaved completely. They don't have any rights. Moreover, they are not only enslaved, they are all the time starved because they cannot work, and all the time terrorized by the army.

And this bleak new Haggadah that Sharon writes, it's written every day here in the newspapers. I don't know how much you know in the States, but here in Israel everybody can read a newspaper and see what happens there. There is no day when a child is not killed somewhere, sitting and eating a sandwich in his house and then getting a bullet in his head.

LS: The Haggadah is the book Jews read during Passover to commemorate escaping from slavery in Egypt. How can you read that with a straight face, or unhypocritically, at a moment in which things are reversed and Israel plays the role of oppressor in the occupied territories? Your line is stunning for that reason. But you also say "Passover is stronger than you are." You're directing that towards the military state. Where do you see the silver lining? In what sense are we going to get out of this?

AS: Yes, I'm still optimistic because I think that evil has no future. Some people here feel, in spite of the PR and the propaganda, that they can't count only on guns and aeroplanes. They also have atomic bombs, but they cannot solve any problem. Only humanism can heal the problems. And Israel is also in an economic crisis. There is no work. So I'm still hopeful because I know that only humanism, only the love between all the people here in the land, between Arabs and Jews, it will come because it's the only solution. It's not that I'm against Israel. It's that this is the only way to survive, because we live here, we don't live in New Jersey, or near Mendocino or Los Angeles. We live *here*, among the Arabs. And the only way is to live together with the Palestinians, and they will be our bridge to the other Arab countries, to be part of the Middle East. And you can see that all these governments that run this system, this occupation, they don't find any solution to any problem here in Israel. So I'm sure, and I hope also, that sooner or later we will have to change. The only hope is the values of Passover. The real values of Passover are the only hope for us to regain our identity as Jews, and also regain our right and our legitimacy in living here. And also building something here, because now it's ruined, literally ruined. Everything is ruined here.

LS: I gather from what you said about you're not being in Mendocino or New Jersey, that there's a way in which the uncritical support of the American Jewish community for Israel is, from your point of view, disastrous.

AS: Yes, they think that they help us, but it's just the opposite. In America, they live more or less in a democratic country, where they live with Irish, with German, with blacks, and they enjoy a society that's relatively healthy, that has human rights, and they demand of us to live on assault all the time. As it is now, we don't see any future of peace here. And they think that they help us if they promote these aggressive ideas and help these policies, instead of compelling us and helping us to find ways to our neighbors that really want peace. But of course, peace without occupation. We cannot take their land and not give them anything, as is being done now. They wanted 20 percent of historic Palestine in order to make peace with us, but nothing was given to them. Not one settlement was closed. I think that the Jews in America, AIPAC [American Israel Public Affairs Committee] and all these groups, are very bad for our future. They think that they help us, but they turn Israel into something without a future.

LS: It's an observation that isn't made often around here. Many people who criticize Israel are automatically accused of anti-Semitism. It doesn't even matter if one is Jewish, sometimes the charge is still made. Of course there's real anti-Semitism, but there's also this phony anti-Semitism . . .

AS: It's not anti-Semitism. It's a constructive way to build an Israel with a future. With a moral way of living, not living like this, like barbarians. What happened yesterday, the killing of Ahmed Yassin, is something completely barbaric. No country in the world does things like this, killing a spiritual leader and then telling lies as if he was really a terrorist. He was a spiritual leader. It's so dangerous now because every Israeli of some rank can also be put into danger. Our leaders are very stupid and very cruel people.

LS: I wanted to ask you if you could read the title poem, "J'Accuse," from your new book.

AS: This poem was written in the beginning of the time of Barak. In a way it's a prophetic poem, because it was really only the beginning. But here in Israel we could know, the Intifada was not something spontaneous, it was planned, and there is also a book about it by Tanya Reinhart. In this book, called *Israel/Palestine*—Seven Stories Press is the publisher—she demonstrated that the Intifada was planned by Barak and Sharon. Sharon . . .

LS: Went to the Temple Mount . . .

AS: . . . and he provoked it. And the terror was only two or three months afterwards. In the first two months, there wasn't any terror by the Arabs; it was only the killing of Arab demonstrators. So then I wrote this poem with a foreboding of what was going to come. It is also about the Oslo time, about what happened before it.

J'ACCUSE

The sniper who shot at Muhammad the child
beneath his father's arm
wasn't acting alone—
someone else in uniform,
a junior cog in the wheel who was briefed
at a higher level,
positioned him there on the roof,
a public servant,
a cantor
for the Days of Awe;
and someone else
manufactured the ammunition,
and another had it distributed

like bars of chocolate.
The tree doesn't go green
when a single leaf unfurls,
many wrinkled brows
leaned over the plans.
History has known
foreheads like these—
technicians of slaughter,
bastards in whose eyes
morality is a pain in the ass.
But even cucumbers
need dirt and a little dung.
The worm isn't born of air;
a million words are required
to reconstruct the manner
in which public discourse itself
is corrupted and turned into refuse—
that which within the body politic
was created to preserve
the heart of justice.

But now
there isn't time for any of that,
when right in front of the cameras,
without any shame,
grown men in uniforms
are shooting into a helpless crowd.
From the back with their necks and behinds
they look like guys at the airgun range
by the screen at an amusement park,
trying to win their girlfriends
a doll or a box of candy.
Atop a hill,
at the distance dictated
by the administrators' handbook,
the prime minister looks on
with his company of advisers.
They gaze down
into the Vale of Tears,

toward the horde which is scrambling
like jackals and rabbits,
grandchildren
and great-grandchildren of refugees
who were stripped of their homes and fields,
wells and towns,
and with an iron hand were driven
into enclaves and ghettos.
Each one of these authorities
sees to his part in the plan:
one's in charge of liquidation,
another of the daily harassment;
this one's field is public relations,
that one's collaboration;
this one deals with expulsion and fencing,
that one with the destruction of homes.
Because, when it comes down to it, we're only speaking
of a population of a certain size,
which needs to be pounded and ground
then shipped off as human powder.
The outrage itself has to be packaged
like any piece of merchandise,
with all the clichés
of corporate politics:
they'll give it a name,
then a format can be arranged
for staged negotiations,
with "breakthroughs" and "concessions,"
and moments of press-covered heightened tension,
complete with a pr blitz full of talk:
for this purpose we have the spokesman,
the journalist and author as well,
the TV announcer and the professor,
a long lineup of Men of Letters,
all blowing into the Process's trumpets—.
For the sniper who fired at the child
is only a single stinking instrument
within an enormous orchestra,
which is conducted by the man who knows

more than anyone else
that long-term solutions can be found
for any and every problem,
when it's no longer breathing.
The moment that man smiles,
the skin over skulls becomes transparent;
when, hoarsely, he pronounces
the word "Peace"—
mothers wake up trembling;
he knows that words
are only the skins of potatoes
with which the stupid are to be stuffed—
and now, at long last,
he'll roll up his sleeves
and get down to the work at which he excels,
and bring about a blood bath.

LS: It's a devastating piece of writing, Aharon. In terms of unveiling the whole system of exploitation, the kind of false language that is produced to veil and conceal what you see as actually going on. The "he" at the end of the poem refers to Sharon?

AS: It was referring to Barak, but as well to Sharon, because Barak is a disciple of Sharon and so the poem keeps its actuality, because Sharon continues and exceeds Barak.

LS: The next step forward in a process of—you use the phrase "ethnic cleansing." It's really hard to come up with a vocabulary that actually matches the specific atrocity we're discussing, and thus attempt to intervene. Yet, Aharon, I'm heartened by your sense of optimism in the long run. Any last thoughts you'd like to leave with in terms of the moment, the present situation, your writing, and anything beyond that?

AS: I wrote a poem called "Hope" but I don't have it in the book. But maybe next time I'll read it. The activity near the fence, there's something new in it. Maybe you don't know in the US, that for the first time young Israelis, many of them, are fighting against the wall together with the Palestinian peasants. It's the first time now that the action for peace and for equality is managed together by groups that completely form one group. And this activity, this common work, which began last year and still continues—every day there are protests near the fence when it is built in new villages—gives me a lot of optimism. This is hope, this is really hope.

LS: I'm calling you from studios at the Evergreen State College. We had a student, Rachel Corrie, who was engaged in work in Rafah, trying to prevent house demolitions and she was run over by a bulldozer, in fact murdered by a soldier on a bulldozer. Have there been casualties yet around the walls, in terms of . . .

AS: Only wounded. The day before yesterday, a young Israeli was wounded near his eye but his eye was saved. In the interview, it said that everybody could see that they shouted, "Don't shoot! There are children here!" It was a protest with many children and many old people and old women and also some Israelis from the Jewish side. And the army shot them with rubber bullets. And one, as I told you, one was wounded. But also, a few months ago, another one was wounded, more gravely, in his leg. Usually the snipers shoot either in the eye or in the leg because they don't want to have a big number killed. They prefer to wound. And people who are wounded are sometimes also lost because in that situation, somebody who loses his eye or his leg cannot continue effectively to live.

LS: Aharon Shabtai, your writing and your role as witness in the present moment of extreme political violence is crucial. Thank you so much for spending this time with us.

2004

On the Politics of Love

If Freud's *Civilization and Its Discontents* remains a master text for our own myth-making, as a section of the following conversation with philosopher Michael Hardt asserts, then it also follows that the relationship between speech and writing remains particularly fraught. Since speech as cure is the most basic assumption of Freudian psychoanalysis, and writing—well, writing is many things for Sigmund Freud and for the rest of us, but surely most of those things are troublesome—then there is an implicit risk in making over speech as text. Writing is the sign of a problem with speech, a problem that speech could not solve for itself, be it a quandary of memory, of authority, of self-reflection, or of an increasing complexity that frustrates speech, for which language as text becomes the objectification and sign. (Socrates, the other end of the spectrum in the discussion concerning Eros that follows, famously refused to write, seeing speech as the vehicle of truth and writing as its loss.)

The psychic sublimations and repressions required in order to write need no review here, though the temptation to remind oneself that Moses wanted us to worship the Writing on the Tablets he had brought; that Freud asks us repeatedly to reflect on Moses; and that Schoenberg's *Moses und Aron* dramatizes for us both the failure of speech (Moses's speech impediment, Schoenberg's idea of *Sprechstimme* in lieu of full-throated song) and the failure of Commandments to sway any crowd the way image, sound, and light can sway us—a temptation that proves irresistible. Freud and Martin Buber, who also comes up in the conversation, came from Vienna, one of the great café cultures of its time, in which, as in all great café cultures, speech is virtually deified. I want to say then that speech, conversation, or dialogue are where we need to turn our attention since it is where our own culture fails us: Starbucks is not the sign of a great café culture, to say the least. The reigning models of conversation, from talk radio to National Public Radio, offer bombast and sterility as our major and minor modes of address. When Holly Melgard and I transcribed the Hardt talk, we wanted not only to maintain its conversational moment, but also to clear away a certain stumbling (on my part of course), so that the reader wouldn't have to stumble with me. Just as the reign of radio mandates the clearing away of most fascicles, the reign of writing clears away one's own disarticulations. In speech, we must struggle through the valley of the letter "u," as in "um," or "um" again, or "uh," and "uh" again, starting from one high point (the impulse to speak), descending down that slightly curved line into the gut, umbilicus, vulva, or underground universe at the bottom of "u," then rising back up again to the peak on the other side of the letter, in what we have brightly said or written, after risking that very inarticulate, "I I" and "u" do that to you—"v" especially, as the concept of love as a political concept discussed here demonstrates.

Speech, more speech, speech offered to speech, with its stumbles and bright spots is, I recognize, the raison d'etre for *Cross Cultural Poetics*, the radio program I've done for five years, interviewing various poets, translators, editors, playwrights, musicians, and philosophers. (Speaking of speech, I don't think "Spoken Word," with all the contempt it heaps on writing, is the answer either, since Spoken Word is never or rarely a spoken word at all, but a highly elevated, highly conventionalized form of address that seems little connected to what one might actually speak, and mostly a monologue at that. Writing seems closer to speech than does Spoken Word.) From whence the transcript of the conversation with Michael Hardt, a conversation now untethered from whatever dramatic circumstance might have originally tied it to speech. Is it a radical political act to have a conversation, when the Internet and other media dependent on writing or image or both, occupy so much of our time, along with commerce itself? A quote from Freud's text: "The aggressive instinct is the derivative and the main representative of the death instinct which we have found alongside of Eros, and which shares world dominion with it. And now, I think, the meaning of the evolution of civilization is no longer obscure to us. It must present the struggle between Eros and Death, between the instinct of life and the instinct of destruction, as it works itself out in the human species. This struggle is what all life essentially consists of, and the evolution of civilization may therefore be simply described as the struggle for life of the human species. And it is this battle of the giants that our nurse-maids try to appease with their lullaby about Heaven." If song qua lullaby is music cleansed of any encounter between two actual beings, infantilizing us, then conversation, still musical but also between beings both actual and imaginary, is the sign of Eros in its mildest sublimation, teetering on its potentially happy, potentially disastrous desublimation.

On Multitudes

An Interview with Michael Hardt

Michael Hardt's recent writings deal primarily with the political, legal, economic, and social aspects of globalization. In his books with Antonio Negri, he has analyzed the functioning of the current global power structure (*Empire*, 2000) and the possible democratic alternatives to that structure (*Multitude*, 2004). He is a professor of English at Duke University.

Leonard Schwartz: You've said that you're interested currently in *love* as a political concept. I wondered if you could say a little bit about that, especially since in *Multitude* (your last book), it does come up. I was speaking with the political theorist Steve Niva who pointed out that it is very clearly there in your piece—in the beginning of the book about the golem. And then, toward the end of *Multitude*, a passage which reads as follows:

> People today seem unable to understand love as a political concept, but a concept of love is just what we need to grasp the constituent power of the multitude. The modern concept of love is almost exclusively limited to the bourgeois couple and the claustrophobic confines of the nuclear family. Love has become a strictly private affair. We need a more generous and more unrestrained conception of love.

Could you comment on that passage and on the direction your thinking has gone since then?

Michael Hardt: In part it starts with a recognition that in certain political actions—in certain political demonstrations, the really good ones—you do have a feeling of something really like love. And so, it's partly a way of trying to theorize that recognition of this feeling of . . . let's call it a "collective transformation" that one experiences in certain kinds of political action. And therefore, to think about *love*, love which I do understand to be precisely a transformative power, something in which we come out different. And to try to think of it as a political concept. There are ways in which love has functioned as a political concept, more than it does today. In fact, when one starts talking about love as a political concept, it's hard to avoid religious traditions. Certainly in Judaic and Christian traditions, love has often been deployed as a political concept, as the construction of the community, precisely. And it seems to me that today, as in the passage you read, that partly through the "segregation" or "confinement" of love into love of the same, love within the family, or even extending further, love of the race. Love of the neighbor was thought of as a restrictive category, let's say. Love of those like yourself has destroyed the possibility of love as a more generous and positive political concept. That's one way thing that has happened. It's the political possibility of love that has been destroyed.

LS: You do bring up the question of the relationship between the form of love that you're theorizing and attempting to describe, and love defined in a religious context. You speak in the *Multitude* of a concept of the new martyrdom (which would be love), but I don't think that is the same as love as a form of sacrifice or the way in which love is worked into a martyrology and sacrificial vocabulary and thought process in religion. I guess I'm asking if you could say a little bit more about how you differentiate between that which you are in the process of articulating and the religious concept of love we have in the West.

MH: I think that once one starts thinking about love as a political concept, it is a dangerous terrain. It is a terrain on which there are many horrible consequences. And I guess I would say that there are many different ways love functions as a political concept, and that some of them can lead to quite horrible ends . . . as I think you're suggesting with the question. I think we have to differentiate between, in one sense "love of the same," "love of the race," let's say "love of the neighbor"—which can be thought of as the same, which can function in a certain kind of nationalism, in certain kinds of religious fundamentalism, and also in which involve exclusion of others—*and* a different notion of love which is the kind of political concept which seems to me we need to create, which is *not* a "love of the same" but in fact a "love of the different," a "love of the stranger." It's hard for me not to repeat certain biblical contexts on this, because I think that within the Judaic and Christian traditions there are a lot of alternatives.

LS: Sure.

MH: But at least that seems to be one division that might be helpful here. On the one hand we have a political notion of love as "love of the same," which functions as a kind of racism, a kind of nationalism, etc., and it does involve love it seems to me. It's important to think of it that way. But, it's horrible. It's "love gone bad," let's say. Whereas, we can think of using that as a caution or a warning: a political notion of love that is not only open to difference—like not only a kind of tolerance, but a love that loves the stranger, a love that functions through the play of differences, rather than the insistence on the same. There's a second criterion one might add to that. As you can tell . . . this is something I'm still in the process of figuring out, so one gets partial formulation of this. It seems to me there's also a horrible form of "love gone bad" in which love is thought of as a merging into one. We get this in Hollywood romances and in romantic poetry, which is when two become one in love. It seems to me to be a horrible idea—both at the level of personal relationships, but also politically. I think rather love has to be thought of as a proliferation of differences, not the destruction of differences. Not merging into unity, but a constructing of constellations among differences, among social differences. Like I was saying when we were talking about religious fundamentalism, we can see the need for thinking about racial differences, the recognition of others, etc. That's another way of distinguishing between love as a political concept that might function democratically, that might work toward a democratic politics, and other ways in which love functions as a political concept, that goes quite wrong. That is a way of thinking about certain kinds of fascism, racialist, nationalist, etc.

LS: I was thinking of Martin Buber who writes and speaks of the love of the stranger. Out of his concept of I/Thou, or on the basis of his concepts that the address between the I to the You springs his notion of a bi-national state that would be Israel and Palestine in one. That was always his argument, that it had to be a single-state solution, that it had to be one state that would incorporate the stranger, be that stranger Jewish or Arab, into a single state. I wondered if Buber is an influence, or someone you're reading. You know, *Multitude* does begin or nearly begin with that image of the golem, the golem is haunting us, drawing directly out of various currents in Jewish mysticism that are not identical to Buber, but certainly related. That section in your book ends with: "Perhaps what monsters like the golem are trying to teach us, whispering to us secretly under the din of our global battlefield, is a lesson about the monstrosity of war and our possible redemption through love." Could you say a little bit about that story of the golem, and why you began your book with it?

MH: On a strictly anecdotal note: my co-author Toni Negri and I, in the kind of games that co-authors play with each other, we had felt frustrated in retrospect that in *Empire* (the previous book), we had used a whole series of Christian theological references. And so, in writing *Multitude*, we thought "Well ok, this time we should have all Jewish theological references." And so we started it as a game that certain kinds of writers play, at least. I'm sure you feel this way, there are certain kinds of constraints that end up being very productive. That's where we started, and so the idea would be then in another book, we would have to have all Islamic references, which is at the moment a little beyond my level of understanding. So we started that way, and it's true that you were referring to Buber and there are a number of authors within the twentieth century Jewish theological tradition who insist on alterity, who insist on that notion of difference as fundamental to any effaceable system. You described it really beautifully too. I think that is something I'm trying to think here. You know, in any number of discussions about difference in political terms, that seems to me to be a very important and operative framework. About the golem: the golem seemed to me a myth of love frustrated and love gone horribly wrong. It seemed to me a kind of cautionary tale like the kinds of things I was just recounting to you, which is that there are certain ways in which we should read these tremendously evil political developments—fascisms, nationalisms, racisms, certain sorts of political fundamentalisms—as forms of love. I mean, I think that they do involve a kind of love. Everyone always talks about them in terms of their hatred, which is of course true too, but I don't think there's really a contradiction between love and hate. What I think is really fundamental to them is there's a kind of "love of the same," "love of the race," and that's what leads so horribly wrong in them. I guess I'm trying to say that the golem was one way of trying to start thinking about this caution about the evils that can result from love gone bad. Therefore, the need to think of the kinds of distinctions, or say, criteria for what would constitute a positive, or productive, or really democratic form of love as politics . . . In a way, starting from there, starting from that caution that you read, it was almost a need or mandate to think further about what would flesh out the notion of "love as politics" in what way of distinguishing that from these quite horrible forms of love as politics.

LS: The golem is traditionally a man made of clay, brought to life by a ritual performed by a rabbi. Golem literally means "unformed or amorphous matter," and its animation repeats, according to the ancient mystical tradition of the Kabala, the process of the God's creation of the world recounted in Genesis. And of course, as you were saying, in most myths or legends of the golem, it goes terribly wrong, and the creation turns against its creator, or the creation is misused by its creator, depending how we read it. When you chose to ground the book in passages from Jewish theology, you described that as part of a constraint-based form of writing. What are the implications? In what ways do you think that shapes the book as the constraint usually does shape the direction that the thought moves?

MH: That was the idea. I think that we weren't as successful as I would have hoped, in the sense of having that consistent reference pervade the thinking. But I think that this particular constraint is one (at least this is what I had in mind) about thinking alterity, of thinking of the notion of difference, or even just thinking the stranger, hospitality. These sorts of concepts seem to me essential to thinking of political movements and political philosophy today. In a way, it guards against thinking of politics as a kind of unification, as the construction of identity that excludes those that are different. There were those constraints or those reminders in thinking about the possibilities for politics and democracy in this age of globalization. That's what I was hoping would be the effect of the constraint.

LS: If I could put another figure in front of you, I would say from the twentieth century Jewish mystical tradition . . . it would be Freud. In *Civilization and Its Discontents,* in that famous passage, in which he describes the couple in love as the most subversive form of energy available, in that the couple in love need no other more sublimated union or form of identification, be it tribal, or ethnic, or nationalistic, or universalist. It's the intensity of that intertwining—not necessarily union—but intertwining that marks that out as potentially destructive of the existing order to the extent that the two don't need any third or fourth or fifth or multitude at that point. I wonder if you could say a little bit about your critique of that notion of Freud. Is that identical to the Hollywood union or the pop song union that of course we're all encircled by? Or, is there something else going on, do you think, in that notion of the sublimated and the "unsublimated"?

MH: Right. No, that's quite brilliant, and I've found—actually you've pinpointed this quite perfectly—in trying to think about this, in trying to think about love as a political concept, I find myself constantly having to struggle with religious theology on the one hand, and psychoanalysis on the other. They're the two boundaries. And it seems ironical for me, because I neither believe in God or the unconscious. I'm not sure which one is a greater violation of some scriptures. In any case, you're right. My first thing to say would be that I think that Freud is not able to think about love outside of the couple or outside of the family. It always comes back to the father, or it always comes back to some primal scene that involves Mommy, Daddy, and Me. That said though, it's true (as you're suggesting) that there is never anything simple in that relationship. There's nothing identical in that relationship that Freud is talking about in love between the couple. There are always—and this is the helpful thing, at least from my way of thinking—an enormous number of other useful things in Freud's thought and psychoanalysis in general, but here in reminding us of the non-identical nature of the way in which there's always multiple meanings in every drive, or desire, or relationship, so that one has to think then of the multiplicity in the relationship. There's nothing purely identical in one's feelings in love. What I would like though—this is the operation that I hope to do—with using the kinds of insights of Freud or psychoanalysis—[to] try to expand them beyond the confines of the familial scene so that we can think further. It seems to me necessary in order to think politically of moving beyond that. It seems to me that Freud always thinks that forms of love that are outside this libido sublimated or frustrated, that the following of the leader is essentially following the father, etc. And so, I think that we need to move outside of that, in order to think of love as a political concept.

LS: In *Multitude* you write:

> We need to recover today this material and political sense of love, a love as strong as death. This does not mean that you cannot love your spouse, your mother, and your child. It only means that your love does not end there, that love serves as the basis for our political projects in common and the construction of a new society. Without this love, we are nothing.

If we look at that passage, are you moving on now to a critique of [normative relationships]? When you say, "this does not mean you cannot love your spouse, your mother, and your child," obviously we can imagine, or we know of positions from which you can't. From a Leninist position that would look at marriage as turning the other into property, from a certain feminist perspective, we can analyze marriage that way as well. You say that, "this does not mean you cannot love your spouse, your mother, and your child." So I'm just asking if you could go a little further into the way in which that is a box that you state in the book, but also OK.

MH: That's great. What I would say is, in a way, love has been destroyed as a political concept. This is a further one, other than what we were talking about before: the personal and political levels of it, or Eros and what's often called Agape, are separated or segregated, so that the "love of the spouse," the "love of the child" that functions on that level of Eros, is separated from the level of "love of the people," which belongs, like you say, to a certain ascetic socialist and communist tradition that's very priestly in that way: refusing the level of Eros and only insisting on this level of Agape, which translates in these political terms into a "love of the people." It seems to me that in order to think of love as a political concept, we have to think it simultaneously as both, that recognizes the connection between and continuum between that level of the personal and the political. The terms don't exactly work here, but at least that is the first way of thinking about it.

LS: Are deployments of the concept of Eros earlier than Freud useful for you in terms of your account of or construction of the political idea of love?

MH: They are . . . It's complicated . . . This is my own philosophical training that's stopping me from speaking at the moment, because when one thinks "Eros," first one thinks about Plato writing about love using the term "Eros," and then about Freud, and they are of course not identical, those two. The way Eros has come to be used most commonly today is primarily in that intimate either familial scene or the scene of spousal coupling, which is segregated from the political. That is exactly what seems to me to be the problem. If Eros could be attached to what would need not deny those energies and let's say, "we need to be revolutionaries in the way in which we care about each other," or something like that. You can imagine the absurd caricatures of that, which unfortunately in some ways, in certain times, have been somewhat true. So, it's not to deny that level of the personal attachment of the love we have for each other, the love we have for those immediately around us, in order to love the people in some abstract sense . . . but neither to limit love to that scene of the personal, and in a way, discount it from politics by saying, "Oh well that's just the personal." It seems to me not an easy operation, but one that's necessary in order to do this, is to think of the two together: the love of those around you and the love of the people. It's both concrete, therefore, and abstract at the same time. I'm not sure if this is making much sense. I at least see it as the problem that one has to confront.

LS: In *Multitude* you do offer a number of examples. In this passage you write:

> We need to invent new weapons for democracy today. There are indeed numerous creative attempts to find new weapons. Consider, for example, as an experiment with new weapons, the kiss-ins conducted by Queer Nation in which men would kiss men and women women in a public place to shock people who are homophobic, which was the case in the Queer Nation action held at a Mormon convention in Utah. The various forms of carnival and mimicry that are so common today at globalization protests might be considered another form of weaponry. So, obviously in terms of the task of writing here to align love with weapons seems, on the one hand, a kind of shocking opposition—though, I guess, we do have Cupid with those arrows and so on, in the tradition. So, I shouldn't be so shocked . . .

MH: *(Laughs)*

LS: You cite kiss-ins at demonstrations by Queer Nation.

MH: Right. In these kinds of political discussions, it's always difficult giving examples (or not always), but often the examples seem to deflate the argument, if you know what I mean.

LS: Yes indeed! *(Laughs)*

MH: It's necessary, but then they seem to bring it down to something very specific that doesn't apply to other things. Those do seem to me to be good examples of struggling against certain norms: of heteronormativity, of certain social structures that prevent love from functioning as a political concept. I think you're right also to point out that once one thinks that love is a political concept, one cannot think love as opposed to or outside of violence. I think that it necessarily involves a certain kind of violence, often a violence against what hinders its actions. It's difficult to give a sufficiently general example of what that would mean: a kind of love that acts through violence. For those who do think in terms of religious scriptures—the Judaic and Christian traditions are full of that—are full of love that requires a violence in order to defend itself, in order to continue as action. I don't mean by this at all that we should either repeat scriptural actions or that we should take the scriptures as models for living, but at least the reference to them sometimes helps because it can denaturalize the current assumptions: for instance, in this case, the assumption that love would never involve any sorts of violence.

LS: There are two things I want to say. One, maybe the most concrete thing we could say, or maybe the most concrete thing I could ask would be, what do you see as the primary barriers that prevent us from actualizing this love?

MH: We've been talking about some that are very important and quotidian, you know, that have to do with everyday life. One attempts to talk about the kinds of practices that do struggle against love that expands beyond the family. This is the way I understand a lot of either what goes under the labels of queer theory or queer practice. Even certain practices of say, gay male cruising that was common in the 1980s, or certain theorizations of that, which I think are trying to struggle against, break the limitations of a certain necessity for love to be confined within the couple. That seems to me to be extremely important on one level of thinking. On another much more important level of thinking, it would probably be better to return to the contexts that you posed earlier, with respect to the golem. One thing that prohibits us from loving the stranger—from enacting the kind of politics that is based on love in a much more general expansive way—is precisely the regimes of violence in the world and those proscriptions for division that prohibit us, that not only make it dangerous, but make it impossible for us to form a politics constructed through love in this way.

LS: The context or *contact*, I should say, between the concept of violence and the concept of love on the one hand, and opposition on the other is, I think, also there in *Multitude* when you write about two different forms of martyrdom. The one form, which is exemplified by the suicide bomber, poses martyrdom as a response of destruction, including self-destruction, to an act of injustice. The other form of martyrdom, however, is completely different. In this form the martyr does not seek destruction but is rather struck down by the violence of the powerful. Martyrdom in this form is really a kind of *testimony*—testimony not so much to the injustices of power but to the possibility of a new world, an alternative not only to that specific destructive power but to every such power. The entire republican tradition from the heroes of Plutarch to Martin Luther is based on this second form or martyrdom. This martyrdom is really an act of love; a constituent act aimed at the future against the sovereignty of the present. I wonder if you could take us through that passage a little bit—in terms of the concept of martyrdom you're describing.

MH: It's nice the way you do these things, because sometimes when you repeat things to me, they sound a little bit more coherent than they did before I heard them.

LS: When I read passages from your book?

MH: Yeah, it's nice.

LS: That's great. I'm glad to be able to provide you that coherence! *(Shared laughs)*

MH: I think you're right, that what's at stake in this . . . there are a couple different things that are at stake. The one is that there is one form of martyrdom, the former one, which is not aimed at constructing anything. It has a certain glorifying nobility in that willingness to die in order to document an injustice. I think from the perspective of the martyr, it functions that way. But the second kind of martyrdom is different in the sense that it's striving to construct a different kind of world, and its martyrdom is not in any way intended, it is a consequence, it is a *risk* that is taken in trying to construct a different world. It is struck down precisely by the forces that don't allow that change to take place. I remember Toni and I, when we were thinking about this, we were making lists for ourselves of all the different historical figures that are considered martyrs, and putting them on one side or the other. In a sense, what we are also doing in a way is protesting against that former type of martyrdom. It seems too often now the martyr has only been relegated to that former figure. We're forgetting there's the sort of figures of martyrdom which were, in a way, bearing testimony, in a way, to a future world, because that's what they were struggling for. They were only struck down in the process before that could be achieved. They're both, I suppose, testimonies—but ones that are pointed in different directions.

LS: So that figure of the martyr is there. I don't think you've set it up as the only possibility that the person who pursues or embodies the form of love you're articulating necessarily ends up martyred—although it is future tense at the end of the book. You say, "This will be the real political act of love." It is something that is, I wouldn't say messianic—although you say there's a Jewish theological kind of weave in the book—but it's still something we're anticipating. This *will* be the real political act of love. Yes?

MH: Yes. I mean it just seems useful to recognize that there are many instances of democracy in the world or attempts toward democracy in the world, but we've not yet achieved it. There's a strong relationship between this act of love as politics, and the coming of democracy for the first time.

LS: I have long thought that the real problem with Christianity is that it hasn't happened yet, and I wonder if that is also part of what's being articulated in your book. But Michael, I want to ask you a question about composition and about the way you work as a writer. I know you're in process on new work. Anything—without interfering with that process—you can tell us about what form your reflections and actions on love are going to take in the new book with Negri?

MH: I think that actually in the book he and I are writing together, love will probably again have a rather limited role. A number of things I have been writing about have been separate from the collaboration . . .

LS: I see.

MH: We go through different phases, as I think any writer does. A previous phase we felt was very important was to try to write in such a way as to engage a larger public and speak in a vocabulary and in a mode of discourse of writing that would be accessible to more people. At the moment, we're in a different phase. We're very much wanting to write for ourselves. Not that we want to be incomprehensible or something, but there are certain problems that we are anxious to work out, and the writing process is the means of doing that. We're trying to give ourselves just the freedom to write just the way we speak to each other . . . if that makes sense.

LS: Absolutely. And love? Are those essays you're working on, or talks?

MH: It's taken mostly the form of the talks now partly because it's a topic that is not yet written because I'm not yet sure how to resolve it, in a way. It is an open question that I don't feel yet ready for. On the other hand, it is a wonderful way to engage people with love, because it is something that doesn't require special knowledge—or in fact there are so many special knowledges that come to bear on it, that everyone has a way of entering into the question. So, I've found it a really wonderful way to open it as a discussion with different kinds of groups. As you can imagine, activists—especially a young generation of activists—I find very appealing, and I find already very natural in a way to talk about political organization and love. In fact, more so than I would say than political activists of my own generation—those in their twenties rather than in their forties let's say. And on the other hand, academics who of course get a little bit squirmy when I start talking about love, because it feels sentimental, it's not quite . . . it's the thing that poets ought to talk about, and not political philosophers.

LS: Yeah, what are you trying to do, take it away from us?

MH: *(Laughs)* But then, once one works through the ideas a little bit, it's embedded in so many of the scholarly fields that people are working on today, that it becomes a very fruitful discussion—and fruitful for me in particular. I guess this is the selfish part of choosing a topic for lectures: it is something that gives me a lot . . .

LS: That's the passion of it to pursue as a philosopher with a love of knowledge and so on. And of course one thinks of, you know, constructing the terms that then can be known in the world. So, when we kidded about stealing something from poetry, that makes some sense, right, to think of the act of creating the object that then can be understood or known. The philosophical or poetic functions form a *couple* in order to accomplish this kind of writing. Don't you think?

MH: Absolutely. And I mean there are long poetic traditions of using the romantic couple as metaphor for the poetic process, and recognizing love as a way of thinking of the process of construction that poetry is. I was thinking of Dante and the Provençal traditions—thinking of romantic love as an analogy of the poetic process itself.

LS: That is a rich source to draw from. The poet Robin Blaser certainly draws deeply from Dante in order to construct a notion of a possible public world, on the basis of a notion of love.

MH: You're right that I should think more about contemporary poets in this regard, because I think that that would be very helpful.

LS: I think that you would find it in the work of Robin Blaser in particular. In his book *The Holy Forest*, his notion of the private as the privy, reduced to the privy, or we're all in a certain kind of privy and the public world that is made accessible or possible through something that he is drawing out of Dante, I would say. So, I was just struck by that reference that you made. As far as a book from you on love goes, we're going to have to anticipate it, is that right?

MH: I think so.

LS: Thank you so much Michael and let's speak soon.

MH: Great.

2007

After Rumi

Don't go anywhere without me.
Say that sort of thing to squirrels
but they'll still scamper up trees,
        not down your tresses,
it's just the way they are.
Or in the grass, in this world or that
location under the grass, you can say
"don't go" there. Better say
nothing. Language
says nothing about it.
Squirrel, I never spoke.

Don't go anywhere without me.
You can say it to your mallet while you work
but your mallet keeps on swinging
once you've gone to sleep,
your tongue keeps moving
once you think you're through conversing.
Words go all kinds of places
and leave me home only when they want to.

Nothing worse than to walk out along the street
don't go anywhere without me.
Don't get onto airplanes, don't go out to restaurants,
don't enter the apartments of other women,
don't go there without me.

More than maps, more than love
don't go anywhere without me.
In case of nuclear attack
don't go anywhere without me.
Our world is coming to an end:
don't go anywhere without me.
Don't go anywhere without me.

Words go all kinds of places
and leave me home only when they want to.
Don't go anywhere without me.

After Babel

The Middle East conflict has shaped a significant part of my writing over the past six years. This is so even though as a poet I see myself as lost in the forest of language; even though it is the voice of the poem that is heard in one's texts, not the voice of the poet; even though I think one should never guide the content or stick to the path of a pre-designated subject matter; even though one writes in the dark. Yet so often in the adventure of writing, when I am truly lost, where I find myself is at the proposition: "and behold, the Palestinians became the Jews of the second half of the twentieth century, and the foreseeable 21st." By which I mean, it was we, the Jews, who lived by language alone, without land, for two thousand years. Now it is the Palestinians who are synonymous with such life. I am saying something very obvious.

Saying is never really obvious. My 2007 chapbook *Language as Responsibility* assumed the necessity of an address to the other. Jewish philosopher Emmanuel Levinas suggested that the very presence of language implies the existence of an other, and therefore each utterance we make carries weight in the world: utterances that stand as if face to face, where the human face proves the existence of the other. From this premise, *Language as Responsibility* combined three forms of address to the other: conversation, proposition, and poem. The first section was an interview with the Israeli poet and peace activist; Aharon Shabtai, the second, an essay on Arabic and Israeli writing in translation; the third section, one of my poems. In the poem I misquote the great Russian poet Marina Tsvetaeva. Early in the last century she wrote, famously, "all poets are Jews." She meant that as poets we are exiled to language, like the Jews were, and that the work of salvage can only be done by way of words, or with whatever words haven't been wasted entirely. I changed it to "All poets are Palestinians." This is true for Jewish poets above all. We must permit ourselves such provocations, remain open to being provoked, and insist on saying paradoxical things.

We speak in a language that is never obvious. For my 2005 book *Ear and Ethos* I wrote a series of poems for which I decided the constraint would be to only use English words derived from Arabic. The way to dissipate toxic notions like "the clash of civilizations" is not with ball-pen screeds or by assuming the moral high ground, but by demonstrating the falsity of those notions. In English we cannot name a piece of fruit without borrowing from Arabic. Languages are intertwined. There is no clash of civilizations.

The myth of language, as both chaos and wealth, is inscribed in the Biblical story of the Tower of Babel of ancient Mesopotamia, in which the Tower collapses beneath human ambition, or divine jealousy, or both, from whence all human languages come. My prose poem, "The New Babel," grappled with my firsthand experience of September 11, 2001 as those towers fell in NYC, and the range of thoughts, perceptions, confusions, and feelings so stirred in the months that followed. This was a day many deemed a culmination of the so-called clash of civilizations. (It felt like a little Hiroshima, and like being in a bombed out village in Afghanistan several weeks later.)

We speak with one another, thanks to language, or by embracing Babel. On my radio program, *Cross Cultural Poetics*, I speak by phone with poets, translators, and writers from all over the world. Did you know that in America we publish less literature in translation by far than any other industrialized democracy? That in America, 2 percent or so of the books published are translation, while in Germany 50 percent or more are translation? How can we hear the words of the other if the other isn't permitted a hearing? If the other isn't permitted words by virtue of our own inertia in meeting those words half-way? Conflict can be mediated by culture, but only if culture is willing to engage in the cutting-edge conflicts of its own day and age. Our culture is primed, the poets and translators are hard at work. It is the greater part of the publishing world, having given itself over to commodity and corporate culture, that fails us the most. The Middle East conflict challenges us to overcome the terrible limitations on our own capacity to imagine something other.

March 2008

After the Assault on Gaza

Perhaps the greatest moral philosopher to arise from European Jewish culture was the Austrian-born Martin Buber, later a citizen of Israel. Buber was a Zionist. His seminal theological text *I and Thou* remains relevant today, a powerful work in its devotion to encounter, to the recognition of the Stranger, to dialogue. Buber's political writings—over a forty-four-year period—are also very instructive. In a 1929 piece "The National Home and the National Riots in Palestine," delivered as a speech in Berlin two months after the Palestine Riots resulted in the deaths of over 125 Jews, Buber wrote:

> Every responsible relationship between an individual and his fellow begins through the power of genuine imagination, as if we were the residents of Palestine and the others were the immigrants who were coming into the country in increasing numbers, year by year, taking it away from us. How would we react to events? Only if we know this will it be possible to minimize the injustice we must do in order to survive and to live the life which we are not only entitled but obliged to live, since we live for the eternal mission, which has been imbedded within us since our creation.

The passage is suggestive of Buber's "I-Thou" conception in that it calls for one group to imagine itself in the position of the other. At the same time, it is very clear in this passage that Buber, as a Zionist, does not shrink from describing Jewish immigration to the Holy Land in 1929 as an eschatological and moral calling, a historical coming-to-pass in the name of which injustices may have to be committed.

With this quote in mind, it becomes doubly instructive, in view of the contemporary situation, to remind ourselves of a text Buber wrote in 1947, "The Bi-National Approach to Zionism." In this extraordinary essay Buber offers the following:

> We describe our program as that of a bi-national state—that is, we aim at a social structure based on the reality of two peoples living together. The foundations of this structure cannot be the traditional ones of majority and minority, but must be different. We do not mean just any bi-national state, but this particular one, with its particular conditions, i.e. a bi-national state which embodies in its basic principle a Magna Charta

Reservationum, the indispensable postulate of the rescue of the Jewish people. This is what we need and not a "Jewish State."

What a prescient statement to have made in 1947! Although Buber's was not the vision of Zionism that triumphed in 1948, we can on its basis assert there was no consensus within Zionism itself in 1947 that a Jewish majority state was a necessary outcome for Zionism and speculate about how a nation in which Buber's view had triumphed might have instead functioned.

What is incontestable is that Buber, a Zionist, calls for a bi-national state. Only this guarantees Jewish survival and justice for the indigenous Arab population of Palestine. As we watch the two ultra-nationalisms of the current moment battle it out with more than 1350 Gazans and 13 Israeli dead in the aftermath of the fighting, allegations of war crimes and deaths multiplying, isn't it possible we should take up again Buber's call for a single bi-national state? I ask this in the spirit of questioning oneself first, an imperative of self-critique that has been a principle of Jewish survival for millennia. If ultra-nationalisms depend on one another to justify their own deadliness, then it is also true that Buber knew that in Palestine/Israel only bi-nationalism could prevent these events. If such violence as we have seen in Gaza is necessary to preserve the Jewish State as we know it, then Israel's actions in and of themselves have proven that only Buber's vision of a bi-national state can save all parties.

The German-language Jewish poet Paul Celan, the great poet of the Holocaust and a fervent admirer of Buber's, wrote of the "Breathturn," that figure in which one breathes in air and breathes out language. Celan spoke of "Breathturn" on his return to Germany in the late '40s, where it could be said he was literally breathing in the molecules of his incinerated people and breathing out poetry, an act fraught with responsibility to the very air he was surviving on and transforming.

The great Palestinian poet Mahmoud Darwish died on August 9, 2008, a little more than four and a half months before the latest tragedy of his people, the attack on Gaza. Both Celan and Darwish's writings bear a similar kind of existential urgency, a related kind of presence in air. Darwish's poems, given his importance to his people and his translatability into other languages, *breathe witness* to the catastrophe of a particular history.

In "The Death of the Phoenix" Darwish wrote:

In the hymns that we sing, there's a
flute
In the flute that shelters us   .   .
fire

In the fire that we feed
a green phoenix
In its elegy I couldn't tell
my ashes from your dust

So Darwish affirms the intermingling of our very molecules, even as elsewhere in the poem he can evoke two figures like Achilles and Priam briefly taking pause from the carnage to admire one another's nobility. For those who read Darwish's poems, language is breath, in the sense rooted in the etymology of the word "spirit." "Phoenix" is a green oasis in burned out times. In its elegy I can't at first tell my ashes from your dust. But then I must: 1350 Palestinian and 13 Israeli dead—these are numbers that should horrify us if one believes, as we do, that every individual matters. In the names of the poets, let us once again keep in mind Buber's very precise call to our imaginations.

March 2009

Language as Responsibility

A poetics of the Middle East, or a poetics of "The Levant," that older and broader geographical term, from "levare" (to raise), applied to the East for the rising of the sun? Hebrew, Arabic, Turkish, French, Aramaic, Ladino, and Greek all figure, among others, as the rising sun's languages, a list which bespeaks an endless co-mingling, parallel conversation, cross conversation, and confusion—but also a bygone era. "The Middle East," a modern political term, is most associated for us with political realities far less polyglot, where languages and the groups that speak them vie with one another, and often kill each other, as opposed to speaking or assuming their place in the collage. Yet languages do supplement each other, even as political realities tear asunder the people that talk. The philosopher Emmanuel Levinas defined language as a responsibility, because to speak always implies the presence of an other; by speaking we subconsciously affirm a presence outside ourselves to whom we stand in relation. It might also be said that to speak a language also implies the presence of other languages, apparently beyond one's ken, and that the responsibility of one language to another is met through translation. That in the United States fewer books per year are translated into English than are translated into any Western European language by the publishing worlds in those countries speaks to a failure of responsibility, a failure which directly feeds into the political expedient of dehumanizing the other. Meanwhile, the very concept of "The Levant" would seem to have sunk into the sublime inane, to borrow a phrase Annette Michelson uses, meaning to be rendered obsolete altogether.

Or almost obsolete. Ibis Editions, based in Jerusalem, is an example of a counter-tendency in English-language culture that paradoxically affirms the possibility of a Mid East beyond the Mid East. Since 1998 Ibis has published ten books in English translation that in their unlikely juxtaposition provide a glimpse into a Levantine reality that offers something other than the images from Baghdad we see televised for our benefit on a daily basis: explosions, technical gadgetry, the eclipsing of one flag by another, war as the basic standard of communication and expression. For the very reason that English is the triumphant language on the world stage—as well as the language hijacked by the warmongers in the Bush administration—these Ibis juxtapositions become crucial. Their list is impressive. (*Revealment and Concealment: Five Essays* by Haim Bialik, the first great poet in modern Hebrew, was for example an important book.) The three founding publishers—Peter Cole (a poet and award-winning translator of Ibn Gabirol and Shmuel Hanagid), Adina Hoffman (author and film critic for the *Jerusalem Post*),

and Gabriel Levin (poet and translator)—have accomplished something that com-
pares to *The Evergreen Review* and *Grove Press* in the 1950s in New York, but in the
midst of a far more conflicted political landscape. The fact that Cole and Hoffman
are Jewish American writers transplanted to Israel is also of interest. What do the
great thirteenth-century Arabic poet Ibn 'Arabi , the influential twenitieth-century
Jewish scholar of Kabbalah Gershom Scholem, and the contemporary Palestinian
poet Taha Muhammed Ali have in common, other than all being published by
Ibis in the last three years? It is the sharpness of the contrast that makes the artic-
ulation of each newly possible, at the very moment that "shock and awe" would
otherwise render us speechless.

    Stations of Desire: Love Elegies from Ibn 'Arabi and New Poems, translated by
Michael Sells, offers a selection of the poems of Ibn 'Arabi. Born in the twelfth
century in Andalusia and known as a master of Sufism, that Islamic form of mys-
ticism, a subject on which he wrote many books, Ibn 'Arabi looms large in the
canon of Arabic poetry. This little volume consists of twenty-four poems from Ibn
'Arabi's book of love elegies, *The Translator of Desires* as well as a selection of trans-
lator Sells's own poems offered in homage to Ibn 'Arabi. *The Translator of Desires*,
or "Turkuman," takes the *qasida*—an ancient Arabic form of poetry dealing with
the separation of lovers—and transforms it into an allegory for humanity's rela-
tion to divinity and the distance between the two that somehow must be bridged
through poetry.

    In his introduction Sells glosses the poetics of it this way: "For Ibn 'Arabi
translation is no word-for-word mechanistic rendition from one system into
another. It is a simultaneous process of 'bringing across' and transformation. In
every moment, the heart must change to receive the new form of the constantly
changing beloved." This formulation is in turn prefaced on Sells's suggestions con-
cerning the mystical dimension of the poetry: "for a Sufi and poet like Ibn 'Arabi,
such a passing away and union with the beloved, though eternal, is also—within
our world of space and time—ephemeral. It is a valid manifestation of the real.
But it cannot be possessed. To try to keep the image of the beloved known in
the union is to freeze it into an idol. The worship of such frozen idols, which
are constructed as "gods of belief" within theologies, philosophies, and religions
leads to a world of mutual intolerance. Each person or group worships the god
of one belief and denies the god of the other. For Ibn 'Arabi . . . such denial is a
form of unbelief. The only true affirmation of oneness is the affirmation of the
one reality in each of its manifestations along with the refusal to confine it to any
one of them."

    Thus what was sacred yesterday is not necessarily sacred today, since the sen-
sation that provokes the sacred can never be frozen, being sensation and not creed.

The political utility of such a tolerant and dynamic notion of the spiritual life hardly needs to be glossed. But how is this awareness activated or made present in the poems? In "As Cool As Life" the text reads:

At the way stations
stay. Grieve over the ruins.
Ask the meadow grounds,
desolate, this question:

Where are those we loved,
where have their red roans gone?
Over there,
cutting through the desert haze.

Like gardens in the mirage,
     you see them,
their silhouettes enlarged
     in the diaphanous mists.

They have gone off seeking
Al 'Udhayb,
     to drink its waters
as cool as life.
. . . .

Their stations will be near.
Their fire will loom before you,
kindling desire
into a raging blaze.

Kneel your camels there.
     don't fear their lions.
Longing will reveal them to you
newborn cubs.

The beauty of these lines is self-evident. Since the beloved is ever-changing we must constantly experience loss. Hence the attraction to ruins, hence the hazy apparitions, hence the new blaze, the violent contrasts between sorrow and ecstatic expectation, water and fire, all at work in the single poem. Indeed, playing off these extremes, Sells own poems in the volume occupy a section entitled "Between the Music and the Graves." (In his "Orisha" "Will you bear these voices/They find you out and are saying//they are your tongue/bluesback echoes of longing . . .) We view fresh ruins with equanimity only should we believe in our missionary rightness in making something better out of those ruins; otherwise they are received in grief, should we intuitively realize that "better" is a euphemism, a phantasm, and that parts of ourselves have just been destroyed. We all live in Baghdad now, more or less, witnesses to a roving destruction we can only fail to distance ourselves from. So too in Ibn 'Arabi's poetry everything that is solid melts not so much into air as into spirit, which for the reader of the poems caught in his own history means into the memory of things sensed but not yet known. Another kind of detachment is experienced too, as if by the translation of desire through the poems one is released from an original belief, which one now realizes was a fetish.

Of course only desire without object would be liberation from the trap. In Ibn 'Arabi's "Stay Now at the Ruins Fading":

I asked her—
when I saw her meadows
now fields of the four
scouring, twisting winds—

Did they tell you where
they'd take their noonday rest?
Yes, she said,
at Sand Hill,

Where the white tents gleam
with what they hold—
from all those rising
suns—of splendor.

"Awe" was originally a religious term, a word one might have previously called upon to suggest the quality of sensation in Ibn 'Arabi's poetry. Now of course it has been transposed by Donald Rumsfeld into a term that refers to the fear that overcomes us in the face of invincible weaponry and prosthetic gods. And "shock"? What was regarded by the early avant garde as an aesthetic value now denotes a silence, a pacification. Can we still use the phrase "the shock of recognition"? Ibn 'Arabi's poems serve to remind us, with a kind of frisson, that there are many rising suns. Poetry—so many words, not a single plastic image—performs its most important feat when it reminds us of the possible.

The revelation that Gershom Scholem was a poet comes as something of a surprise. Scholem of course was a hugely influential scholar. His *Major Trends in Jewish Mysticism* established the field of the modern study of Kabbalah, and his *Walter Benjamin: The Story of a Friendship* remains a secret and surprising book. Cynthia Ozick famously quipped in *The New Yorker*: "He was not a man penetrating a field of learning; he was a field of learning penetrating the world." George Steiner, in that same magazine, wrote, "Scholem is the rarest of spirits . . . He is at once a philosopher, a social historian, a wise and forceful essayist, and one whose conscience this tormented, devious and murderous world has, alas, heard a great deal from, but also has too often ignored." Scholem's name is inextricably linked with Hebrew University, where he was university professor for many years and where he became associated with the proudest traditions of Zionism. And yet during most of these years in Israel he continued to write poems in his native German (he was born in Berlin in 1897 and settled in Jerusalem in 1923), on the basis of which German, too, I suppose, passes into the lexicon of the Levant. Zionism itself a German-Jewish ideal. These poems, along with two originally written in Hebrew, are all collected in *The Fullness of Time*, translated by the renowned Richard Sieburth, and introduced and annotated by Steven M. Wasserman.

The poems are as interesting for what they reveal about Scholem's thought as for what they are in and of themselves. The great scholar of mysticism is himself no mystic. In form, Scholem's poems read like old fashioned nineteenth-century European verses; in tone, they are often either caustic or comic, but never truly ecstatic. Scholem's admiration for a Moses-like Theodor Herzl, father of Zionism, is palpable in the 1915 poem "To Theodor Herzl" and constitutes perhaps the nearest thing to the ecstatic in this book:

We shall never forget what it was he meant,
Who gave us this dream so rich, so glowing,
And who restored what we had once possessed
And what we had lost—without our knowing!

He shouted of a world that rose, amazed
At his words, the words of our own distress.
He held the flag high while the enemy raged,
And the flag was bloody red.

What is surprising about this body of poetry, however, is how quickly in Scholem the dream of Zionism seems to sour. Perhaps one should be less surprised. The vision of Zionism supported by the most renowned of the intellectuals associated with Hebrew University—Martin Buber most especially, with whom Scholem's scholarly work stands in a relation of both indebtedness and contestation—all identified themselves with a leftist Kibbutzim movement that called for a bi-national socialist state of Jewish and Arab workers united in a single political organism. Such was not to be the case, as 1948 bifurcated into the birth of Israel on the one hand and the Nakbah (Catastrophe) on the other, a partition (though only one state was formed), which has proven to be a nightmare for all peoples involved. Consider the mood of Scholem's poem "Jerusalem," written in that city in the summer of 1948, in the midst of the War of Independence:

> you sense that all the age-old life pent
> up in this city now draws to an end,
> and you know: she is now spent,
> expended on the Real, and commences
>
> to detach herself from the present.
> Poor, dethroned, stark in her nakedness,
> she stands there, whom enemies could not sway,
>
> and is once again what she always was:
> a mere memory of a former greatness
> and a waiting for the Final Day.

Does this poem bemoan and anticipate the fate of a divided city, or imagine, messianically, some future end to history, or simply capture a mood of anxiety and dread? I would suggest there is a grand disappointment here concerning the very notions of return that had been so passionately embraced in the 1915 poem "For Herzl." After all, in 1948 the Levant was on the verge of being split. A third horror, following the Holocaust and the Nakbah, was about to follow: the mass expulsion of Arab Jews from Iraq, Iran, Yemen, and elsewhere in the Arab world, in retaliation for the expulsion of the Palestinians from the new Israel (in many of these places five hundred years' worth of Jewish community and cultural life almost entirely obliterated). As early as 1921 Scholem had written, in a letter from Munich, of "the fatal modern conflation of religious and political categories that desecrates both, turning them into a game that someday is bound to turn violent." Perhaps Scholem, scholar and witness to history, in this poem plays upon the classical Jewish posture of waiting for redemption from history in a mystical future, after history has ended. Certainly he participates in the proudest of Jewish prophetic traditions in refusing to compromise with the golden calf, to buy into the new fetish of the tribe—vulgar nationalism, the secular posturing as sacred, with the pat solutions nationalism offers to all the contradictions of history.

In his 1967 "To Ingeborg Bachmann, after her visit to the ghetto of Rome," Scholem writes:

Zion's messengers speak to us of elation,
but we can never quite return back home.
Though we once were filled with anticipation,
this call to homecoming cannot be restored.

The message that called us home
reached the ghetto far too late.
The hour of redemption is over,
the final day's decline—too plain.

If Ibn 'Arabi, in his age, had plumbed the flux of sensation in which total loss transforms into divinity in order to relocate the beloved instant by instant in the flux of alienation, then it is tempting to suggest that Scholem, at a critical distance from the mystical tradition he was the elucidator of, nonetheless employed that mysticism to gently suggest not only the inadequacy of the real, but the betrayal of the dream. What horror to suggest that this particular dream has soured, since redemption sours with it, which is to say all those who died in Europe also died in vain. This Scholem never said; publicly he maintained the possibility of a redemptive "left" Zionism. But there is an equal horror whenever those who died in the Holocaust have their names invoked as justification for the next violation, and of this Scholem was also keenly aware. In every moment, the heart must change, wrote Ibn 'Arabi, or the beloved is lost. Scholem died in Israel in 1982.

Never Mind: Twenty Poems and a Story is the first collection in English translation of the poetry of Taha Muhammed Ali, an Arabic-language poet living in Nazareth. Ali was born in 1931 in the Galilee village of Saffuriya. As with other Palestinian poets the constant refrain of his work is the lost paradise of his youth. In his introduction to the poems Gabriel Levin writes:

Saffuriya, or at least the village of the childhood, where myth and reality converged, shone in the poet's mind as a place of prelapsarian innocence and embodied, in Palestinian terms, that period before the "great catastrophe" an-Nakba, brought about by the Arab-Israeli war of 1948 and the consequent shattering and exodus of the Palestinian community. In July of that year, Ali's village, which had sheltered local militiamen, was hit by artillery and then bombed by Israeli aircraft. Most of the villagers fled into the surrounding wadis and orchards, believing that the Arab Liberation Army would come to their defense. But the ALA was not forthcoming, and the inhabitants of Saffuriya dispersed. Some made their way northward, to Lebanon, while others found temporary refuge in the neighboring villages . . . The poet and his family chose the northern route to Lebanon, where they spent a year in a refugee camp before managing to infiltrate back into Israel. By then, however, the IDF had leveled Saffuriya to the ground, and the Israeli authorities had handed over to local kibbutzim thousands of dunams of fertile village land. Like many other former inhabitants of Saffuriya, Ali and his family settled in Nazareth, where he has remained for the last fifty years.

Ali's poems are direct, unpretentious, and disarming, translated into a fluent colloquial English by Gabriel Levin, Yaha Hijazi, and Peter Cole, working in tandem. These poems are not ideological or nationalistic in bent, nor are they learned; the recurring figure of Abd El-Hadi the Fool, a kind of innocent dreamer, undercuts any kind of heroic inflation, intellectual pretension, or fetish. Yet the history is real, and realized in the poems. In "Ambergis" the anger and admonishment against history is cast in terms of an outcry against the bitchiness of the earth itself. The disenchantment/enchantment with the desired land that is home echoes interestingly (in an entirely different register) Scholem's "Jerusalem" (1948):

This land is a traitor
and can't be trusted.
This land doesn't remember love.
This land is a whore
holding out a hand to the years,
as it manages a ballroom
on the harbor pier—
it laughs in every language
and bit by bit, with its hip,
feeds all who come to it.

The colloquial quality of the writing is important too. As translator Levin points out in his introduction readers of Arabic will surely find Ali unusual for his insistence on a specific Palestinian vernacular, over and against a more high flown, windy modality often preferred in Arabic poetry, the kind of modality much more susceptible to an escalating rhetoric (as for example in French poetry). In "Three

Qasidas," for example, Ali adopts the traditional Arabic form to his own particular needs and arrives at, in section one, "Imprisonment":

> When I was free,
> my fear was wrapped
> around my neck
> like a viper!
> And you were the sole
> spring of my sadness.
>
> But now . . .
> the bread of my fear has been depleted
> and the wine of my sorrow
> pours forth from every fountain.

The qasida, adapted to express the distance between matter and spirit in Ibn 'Arabi, here becomes the distance between the speaker and the land to which he speaks, as if the ground of the poem were also the ground in which one's feet ought to be planted—but never are. Thus "ground" is colored as wine, both intoxicating and sad, and words only know the ground's absence. "Postoperative Complications Following the Extraction of Memory" reads the title of another poem. The irony of course is that this poetics of loss, accompanied by or only borne on the basis of a sense of humor, so closely resembles a Jewish one.

The last stanza of "Never Mind," the title poem, is unremitting not only in terms of poet and ground, the particular and the absent, but also about the necessity of address, in Levinas's sense, however bitter that address may be:

> Let me stroll
> within range of your rifle,
> among these deserted gardens
> and ruined stone walls;
> allow me
> to greet this fig tree!
> Let me draw near
> to that particular cactus.
> And then, after the harvest,
> catch me
> and slaughter me
> with the fine threads
> that dangle

from your sleeves and pack
like the guts from a chicken's belly!

Again, the bitterness of the circumstance of address does not exhaust the
speaker entire. In "Abd El-Hadi the Fool":

my great apostasy
is this:
no sooner does the laughter
of a child reach me,
or I happen upon
a sobbing stream,
no sooner do I see
a flower wilting,
or notice a fine-looking woman,
than I'm stunned
and abandoned by everything,
and nothing of me remains
except
Abd El-Hadi the Fool!

Perhaps these lines, in the simplicity of their declaration, serve as well as an
emblem for Ibis Editions quixotic pursuit of a Levant that, at the very least, still
exists within the pages of its books, a Levant in which English too finds its place
as a literary middleman, a zone of cross pollination. Ibis co-publisher, co-transla-
tor and poet Peter Cole is quoted in the *New York Sun* as saying: "the Levant is at
one and the same time a realm of the imagination and a concrete, if rather messy,
melding of cultures, ethnic groups, tribes, religious sects, schisms, heterodoxies,
with porous boundaries." Today in the Middle East the talk is of building walls,
not of porous boundaries. If they build, they build. But in every moment, the very
chambers of the heart must change.

2005

Sells, Michael, and Ibn 'Arabi. *Stations of Desire: Love Elegies from Ibn 'Arabi and New Poems.* Translated
    by Michael A. Sells. Jerusalem: Ibis Editions, 2000.
Scholem, Gershom. *The Fullness of Time: Poems, by Gershom Scholem.* Translated by Richard Sieburth.
    Introduced and annotated by Steven Wasserman. Jerusalem: Ibis Editions, 2003.
Ali, Taha Muhammad. *Never Mind: Twenty Poems And A Story.* Translated by Peter Cole, Yahya Hijazi,
    and Gabriel Levin. Jerusalem: Ibis Editions, 2002.

The Ghetto of Gaza and the Angel of History

Normally a city opens up to other cities, infinite in itself because infinitely open to the world; one moves with a certain freedom through space and imagination. What is it like instead to live and write from inside a ghetto, or an open air prison, or a city closed to other cities, one in which nearly every act of resistance is taken as a pretext by the warders to tighten that very straightjacket? A famous example of such writing comes to us from the great German-Jewish litterateur Walter Benjamin, in his essays written after Hitler's rise to power. Fleeing the Nazis, Benjamin committed suicide near the closed Spanish border, rather than risk being sent to a camp the next day. It was in his "Theses on the Philosophy of History," however, that Benjamin wrote of the "Angel of History." The figure of the Angel of History has been much discussed ever since.

Benjamin wrote:

his eyes are staring, his mouth is open, his wings are spread . . . His face is turned toward the past. Where we perceive a chain of events, he (the angel of history) sees one single catastrophe which keeps piling wreckage upon wreckage and hurls it in front of his feet. The angel would like to stay, awaken the dead, and make whole what has been crushed. But a storm is blowing from Paradise; it has got caught in his wings with such violence that the angel can no longer close them. This storm irresistibly propels him into the future to which his back is turned, while the pile of debris before him grows skyward. This storm is what we call progress.

In our century it is the Palestinians of Gaza who are experiencing mass incarceration of the kind that the Venetian word "ghetto" once meant for the Jews of Europe. We can see this dilemma embodied in the prose poetry of Somaya El-Sousi, a poet living and writing in Gaza City, who is active internationally but rooted in her city. In her recent prose poem "The City" El-Sousi writes:

What will this sad, silent, fallen city by the old sea oppressed by time give you? It will give you a lot if you listen to its nightly voice strewn amongst the rustling of the trees and the lapping of the waves. No one tries to listen to that angelic voice emanating from it. Everyone only hears his own voice and strives to search for himself among the city's heaps . . . Often

I think if only geography wasn't so clever, if only it bestowed the city with a few more coastal kilometers and released it from its existing borders; how would your seashore look, oh Gaza? Which ships would reach you? What would be the State of your residents, teeming with feelings of exile, cries, and fear? Perhaps it is the constant thought of escaping the city's boundaries weighing on me, or at least the idea that my city is without borders, drowning in isolation. A city where whoever enters is lost, and whoever leaves writes himself a new life story. Now there is no leaving and no entering. A city of imprisonment that consumes its own inhabitants and which everyone wants to escape . . .

"The City" comes to us not from the eye of the storm but from the eye of something other—stranger, harder to define, more everyday, though just as unstable as a storm, both more bereft and more hopeful and alive. If it is a storm after all perhaps it is the one Benjamin writes of in his passage on the Angel of History. Certainly the angelic voice El-Sousi writes of is beautiful and grim. It tells of a city of infinite possibilities—reduced to a flat surface. It tells of a place in which one must struggle to hear the rustling of the trees. Yes, the Angel of History is certainly here, facing backwards, contemplating the past in all its bloody injustices as they call out to be righted, or to be avenged. But the Angel is already in flight. And there is something else here too, something other than vengeance or righteous indignation . . .

The difference between Benjamin's text and El-Sousi's lies not only in its perspective on the Angel of History itself—in his text it is an image, in her text it is a voice—but also in the "Never Again" inscribed into the situation of language after Benjamin. When uttered in its authentic meaning this phrase does not mean "never again" the ethnic cleansing of the Jews, but "never again" ethnic cleansing at all. Will the voice of such an awareness yet prevent one specific people from continuing to permit itself to seek such ethnic cleansing under other name?

El-Sousi's haunting words press up against the glass walls of the cyber-ghetto, and the veiled walls of dream, and the actual guns enforcing incarceration and limiting speech and movement in the actual ghetto. As Jewish people we cannot but help recognizing ourselves, or our ancestors. All ages are contemporaneous. Let it not be said Gaza City is not without a human—or an angelic—voice.

July 2009

Interview with Amiri Baraka

Leonard Schwartz: On the back of one of your more recent books, *Transbluesency: Selected Poems 1961–1995*, Arnold Rampersad writes "Amiri Baraka stands with Wheatley, Douglas, Dunbar, Hughes, Hurston, Wright, Ellison, as one of the eight figures who have significantly affected the course of African American literary culture." I wonder if you could comment on the trajectory this proposes and where you see that trajectory going?

Amiri Baraka: People make their own judgments obviously, but I think it's a high honor to be included in that kind of list. These are people that I've always admired and to a certain extent thought of as paradigms. That's a good thing at this point in American history, though there needs to be another kind of Renaissance, another kind of revival—on the Afro-American side, but also on the All-American side. We've reached a sort of impasse in terms of the Postmodern; you can talk about the end of progress, the end of new revelations, but I believe that if that's the case, we definitely need a cultural revolution.

LS: So you see ourselves not at the end of some Hegelian dialectic but someplace in the middle of it, faced by a new conflict?

AB: The arts have to reflect the politics of the period to a certain extent. In the '60s we had a kind of international anti-imperialist movement, and the Civil Rights movement and the anti-war movement here in this country. Along with a kind of vital art, a dynamic aesthetic that reflected the world as it was. It's what Du Bois calls the Sisyphus Syndrome: we rolled the rock up the mountain and they'd roll it back down on our heads. This is definitely the rock rolling down period. Although we have some indications that people might be ready to try to push it back up.

LS: There's a powerful sequence in *Transbluesency* entitled "Wise, Why's, Y's"— can you give us some sense of how that sequence functions?

AB: Well, this is actually from a book called *Wise, Why's, Y's* which is forty poems. Forty because of forty acres and a mule, as in Reconstruction. And also it's supposed to be forty days and forty nights, that trip from Africa to the Western World on the slave ship. But anyway, this is supposed to be a very generalized and abstract history. It begins with a long introduction that includes drums and so forth that I usually make with my mouth. It's called the PRE-HERE/ISTIC Sequence, which is divided into "Dat," which is Africa, drums; "Deuce—Ghost" (Snake Eyes), a piece called "Space Spy"; "Tray—My Brother the King," three-quarter solos, waltz solos, and Dun Dun, just the drums; and five railroads of African bones which is box cars and crap talk and underwater African funeral music.

LS: It's fascinating—and it makes me think about the poet Kamau Braithwaite, who has been a frequent guest on *Cross Cultural Poetics*. I wondered if you could say a little bit about his idea of Nation Language and the idea that one is not, or he is not, writing in English. He's been writing in a new language that emerges out of English, in a revolt against English although it looks like English from the outside.

AB: He's talking about the speech of Jamaican masses actually. There's another important person, Kwesi Johnson, who does that, and also Oku Onura and Mutabaruka. What it conveys is a sense of a people as speech as place—you know, where you get the sense of place through the language you use. It's interesting that they sometimes call it Dub Poetry; if you read a book written in the early nineteenth century called *The English Isles*, you'll find mention of a language called Dub Chaint.

LS: If you think about African American speech, African American language, which is distinctive and original and a place from which new expressions come into American English as whole, but is also quickly commodified, turned into a commodity for middle-class people to use to feel cool . . . what are the particular politics of this language?

AB: I think you framed it pretty clearly! Rap records, even ones that the Black community might object to strenuously, find big sales in white suburbs by young people who want to feel hip, because in the end somebody like Imus, as patently stupid as that is, he thought he was being down with it, you know, he was being down with the people. He thought he could talk like somebody as simple minded as Snoop Dog, but the point is that language is political in the sense that it has users, and its users are usually placed according to the speech that they use. Americans have never spoken standard English, that's a bizarre pretense—the white people that came here, they were Cockneys, Irish, they came from Wales and from Scotland—they used all kinds of languages that they incorporated into American and African speech. You can say that American culture is composed of Africa, Europe, and Native America. It's that mixture; you can't go a lot of places without speaking Spanish, or you have to use Native American language in some places, certainly throughout the Midwest, or if you go down south you find yourself speaking some kind of a Bantu language to describe rivers and mountains. The language is a mixture of its users, but in terms of its politics, to use what's called "Black Speech" is to be diminished economically, though it's still cool as entertainment on the stage. I think that "minorities" always are bilingual. You speak one language in the community with your peers and then you go out of that community to work or whatever and you speak another language.

LS: Peter Quartermain has a book, *The Poetics of Disjunction,* in which he argues that the early roots of the avant-garde tradition in American poetry, and he points to Stein and Zukofsky, were all people for whom English was a second language, specifically Jewish authors who grew up in Yiddish, so that there was a need to distort or transform the language out of the dissonance or conflict between the two languages. Obviously the avant-garde has always faced the issue of what to do when your texts are appropriated or when your structures, tactical and otherwise, are appropriated . . .

AB: Well, it's like an escaped slave, you can't stay in one place too long.

LS: Well, that's it. It seems to me there's such a clear parallel between that aesthetic predicament for the avant-garde and the existential predicament everyone is in.

AB: If you say something this week, by next week it's cliché: when Black folks say something like "I'm outta here," and the next thing you know is Clinton saying "I'm outta here," it makes fresh speech cliché. It's just a faster process of cliché making in the United States, because whatever you say becomes commodified almost immediately. I don't have a problem with that per se, all cultures learn from each other. The problem is if the Beatles are telling me they learned everything they know from Blind Willy John, I want to know why Blind Willy John is still running an elevator in Jackson, Mississippi. It's that kind of inequality that is abusive, not the actual appropriation of culture. I don't think you can have a Duke Ellington without digging Beethoven. And I don't think you can have a Debussy without digging Duke Ellington. And everybody digs each other, what other people do. The question is can they find a standard of living for the use, that's the main thing.

LS: Sure, if cultures are porous to one another that's what makes it possible to be intertwined, but if the terms of that intertwining are exploitative, then there is less an intertwining and more a domination, and then we have the problem. On the question of reception and the way in which things get commodified and appropriated, do you mind if I ask you about the controversy around your poem "Somebody Blew Up America" and the way in which a few lines from that poem were taken out of the context and transformed into a brouhaha . . . was that ultimately a healthy thing, or debilitating?

AB: Well, I just wish they would pay me. The question of somebody calling it anti-Semitic, though, has to be fought. I've gone to court twice and we are preparing to go to the Extreme Court now. That has to be fought because I just cannot accept it. What the poem questions first of all is terrorism, saying that hey, the whole reason that we're in the United States, Black people, is because of the terrorism of the slave trade, the terrorism of the Middle Passage, the terrorism of lynching, the terrorism of slavery. I wrote that poem a month after 9/11. From our house here in the Clinton Hill section of Newark, we can see, or we could see, the World Trade Center from the third floor. I was supposed to go over there that day to help Felipe Luciano with his campaign as councilman. They called me up and said, "Look at the TV." Then backward people start saying it's anti-Semitic. First, this thing about five Israelis on top of the roof photographing the event. Hey, I got that from the *New York Times,* the *Star Ledger,* the *Washington Post.* So I mean, why me? The other question was who told Israeli workers at the Twin Towers to stay home that day? That's simple: call the Israeli Embassy! I'm not talking about Jews, that's what evil people conflate it into saying I said. That's a lie. I said Israelis, meaning Israeli nationals, citizens of Israel. And if you don't think they had some information about that, call the Israeli Embassy! Say "How many Israeli Nationals died in the World Trade Center?" They'll tell you four: two in the plane and two in the building. If you also check the *Wall Street Journal* about tenants at the World Trade Center on 9/11 you'll find that there are many, many, many Israeli Companies. OK, this is where people are saying you're saying that Israel had some knowledge about that? *Israel said that.* You can read that in *Haaretz,* you can read that in the *New York Times.* They said they've warned the United States, and not only Israel but Germany, France, Russia, all said they warned the United States about that. The other thing is this: all states, all countries warn their nationals when they're in a situation liable to put them in jeopardy. That's the normal thing: don't go here, don't go there, there's a warning, stay out of Iran, stay out of Lebanon. So that's what Israel said to their workers in the Trade Center. That's a normal function of the state. And to say that somehow that makes me an anti-Semite, that's wacky.

LS: To me it is clear reading your poem that there are sections—"Who killed the most Jews? Who killed the most Italians? Who killed the most Irish?"—in which there's a concept of the Jewish as a certain kind of victim of history that runs through the poem, and that's very much in distinction to the concept of Israel, which is a nation state.

AB: That's right, but the way that Israel defends itself, which is shrewd to a certain extent, is by cloaking itself in Judaism. If you question Israel, you're putting down the Jews. That's crazy! I should be able to say something bad about Africa without putting down Black people. I think that all this murder using religion as a shield, whether it's Judaism or it's Islam or Christianity, is just nonsense. As a matter of fact, one of the most dangerous religions in the world today is Christianity, in terms of killing the most people.

LS: It's so rare for a poem to take on a public kind of status or object of debate the way that "Somebody Blew Up America" did. I'm wondering, although I'm sure it was personally painful and upsetting to be under that kind of attack, whether ultimately you found it useful for a poem to be able to produce that kind of effect in the commonweal?

AB: When I was younger I read a book by David Walker called *The Appeal* that was written about 1829, and I thought, if I could ever write a poem so terrible that people would ban it, and be sentenced to jail for reading it . . . I didn't know I could actually do that. There was a poem I wrote in '66 called "Black People" that in 1967 the judge used as a reason to sentence me to three years in prison. He said that the poem was a prescription for criminal anarchy. And I wanted to know, Judge, do you mean that people came in my house and read that poem before they set fires during the Newark Rebellions in '67? That's the kind of emotional reaction that poetry can make.

LS: Your book *Somebody Blew Up America* came out as a book with a publisher in the Caribbean, The House of Nehesi. Are there other works we should be looking for in the near future?

AB: I published a book called *The Essence of Reparations* (2003) that came out with Nehesi. It's interesting that the publisher was a student of mine at SUNY Stonybrook—he graduated and went home and started a publishing company.

LS: That's amazing. That's the kind of student one wants.

AB: This young man, Lasana Sekou, was recently knighted by the Queen of the Netherlands. They have some kind of relationship with the Netherlands, in Saint Martin. So now he's Sir.

LS: My goodness. Is that intimidating, to refer to your publisher as Your Lordship or Sir?

AB: I don't know, he still calls me "Teacher."

LS: Oh, that's good. Students aren't respectful enough often enough these days, don't you find?

AB: (chuckling) Yeah.

2007

The Eden Exhibit

1

The Eden Exhibit had already left town. But because I live here and have received instruction I recognized in your enthusiasm, striving towards the world, some trace of the unfettered energy one might have seen displayed there, hung in effigy.

2

Alive in a city of varied cuisines, on familiar terms with both its subways and its goats. You stare into the fisherman's bucket, nothing caught; copters hover low in search of god knows which suspect. Military in the streets, passing us as though they were already smoke and not sons and daughters, as if we had all gone up in smoke with them, all us voices gusting like ghosts between the power lines.

3

The city certainly has changed. Of course at each moment it was I who defined the limits of what I knew. Symbols contain emotional force but they are as much worm food as are these hands. All depths stream darkly muffled utterance. Then your voice calls me back to the immediacy of the alphabet, to a music rising ever again from the moment I had so fecklessly abandoned. What did you just say?

4

More and more free, like kites torn loose, each passing dog eliciting a cry of excitement. It is true that with love there are no strings attached. Breezes offer each other a secret sign.

5

Up a belated ladder, beginning to wonder is that a lake or a fog, an A or a D streaking up the tunnel? I've always felt anxious in supermarkets but you don't seem to notice; the whole lives only in its individual moments. And the physical separation between urban living and the land itself is supposed to be transcended by the presence of the park, these very grounds we now traverse, moving west to east, from golden horses to real ones of various adornment and color. Things sayable only to one who perceives things as such, in consonance with a source also mine.

6

Sometimes I must seem hard to you, the stars gathering and glittering in your eyes bursting with focus. Wash your hands, eat your noodles, pick up the clip, and so on.

And all the while the bomb continues its downtown countdown. One, two, three, four, five, all gone. What is the name again of the city we live in? Our single shipwreck, the vanishing floor—a billiard ball tumbling from a newspaper and landing in the exploded room below.

7

The victors are served wine preserved in the mouth of a dead mother, signification itself the moment of violation. Each year makes up a new explanation. Each of us missing a chunk of name, or of brain, fences looped along the borders of identity, your toothless compatriots crying and crying and crying.

8

A man brings a bicycle aboard the A train. You point it out. I concede that a bicycle on a subway car is incongruous, though I've seen it many times before: the shiny metal, the motionless spokes, the silenced horn. This will be a short ride. We are going our separate ways.

9

That afternoon, months before, walking along 16th Street, when I was overcome by the imprecise news of precision bombing, the proudly announced intention to decapitate, and cried live tears. How was I going to tell you about this, you who are already a veteran of these wars without even being conscious of them, you who are aware of each passing horse in the heart of the metropolis, so deeply in tune with the agrarian in the urban, the Rhinegold at the bottom of the Rhine?

10

Remember that time police cars converged, sirens blaring? I said, Forget the bus, lets grab a cab and get out of here. Let's get kicked out of a bar together, when they change the rules and don't permit kids to listen to the crooner. Let's scoff at the two year olds being wheeled in carriages, those glazed expressions pasted up and down their faces.

11

I'm talking about something like that, that day they began the bombing. But you know, I'm also here with you. Not even the slightest shadow encroaches upon this noon of encounter. Each corner articulate with particular impression, each musician that takes to the street that street's anima chivvied into expression. Every event is beyond prediction.

12

The nail of an idea goes into the plank of stupidity. But there is no guarantee that what will be built will not also be stupid. Just look around you. You do, and announce you want to build buildings, in spite of the power drills whose scream you scurry from. Conversant with poets and singers and doctors too you select " to build buildings," and also " to farm cheetahs." To raise cheetahs, right? Yes, that's right, to farm cheetahs, to farm panthers, to farm panthers and cheetahs. Fine, I will support you in those endeavors. We haven't been to the galleries lately. Let's run for it.

Red Fog

A red fog occupied both the cities and the hinterlands.

After the collective memory of a time before the fog begins to miniaturize itself, turning into a key that slips from a parents pocket while playing with his child in the grass; after the wild grasping hands of beings unlike ourselves withdraw into the wood; after the absolute alarm of flesh succumbs to the infirmity of the mind in its failure to imagine flesh alight; after the alabaster alarm clock of the self began to ring and ring and ring—deep in what sleep, deep in what sleep?—or after the words have bedded down for the night; after the night unfurls over the empty headlands and the wind offers ultimatums to the exhausted sand: after the laughter of the ocean shakes the fulcrum of my being; after the rain cloud exhausts every drop of its discharge and exists only as kneeling puddles and slinking eddies sinking ever lower on the plain; then, a spiral motion.

You believe in perceptions, in forms, in bodies, in perceptions of forms and bodies, but these are all maps, the perceptions, the bodies, the forms. You choose to look at them—the bodies and the forms—but there are no maps onto which to place what you see, no charts with which to freeze what you feel, no maps or charts to deploy in order to traverse or conquer this field. The word "map," like the word "God," a vile obscenity. This obscenity fills my work with spiral voids. A cat chases a red point of light shot from a pointer, a moving beam impossible to paw, impossible for pussy not to pursue: red beam projects red point, red beam traceable back to held pointer, a watch in the sand by the shore. Words are beamed without point. Thus she chose to remain wordless, would not utter a single sound. She spoke. Thus, a spiral motion.

After the city had been abandoned and the dog had begun to bark, after the conversation with difference ended, the limp that came in and the imp that went out; after the gaps between "A" and "B" and between "C" and "D" failed to reveal any unsuspected images and sounds; after self-contemplation was reconfigured as elf immolation, the well-spring of pent-up waters left so pent, or allowed to rush as inexact vocabulary into an immovable glacier, tense with the effort that drives off what I intended to maintain by effort, relaxing and letting drop what I intended to preserve, doubting in the words I helped elicit in the other, the one I was speaking to and helping to speak and investing my own energy in the speech of. In other words: am I a man dreaming I'm a spiral motion, or a spiral motion dreaming I'm in dialogue? The heart-held camera only shows us what it wants to show us in any given beat.

After the rabbit had been eaten and the cigar burned so low it refused to be relit; after switching one word with another word and watching them both burn up in their new locations; after the mind failed to fill in the space around it with an aesthetic of its own compulsion; after the words had become weighted with their worst associations, yet still were recognizable as what they had been before and thus did not become new words; after the furrows in the field were covered with frost; after the frost was speckled with some dark spore released by the action of the frost working upon the field; after a mouse, trembling, exited from his hole into the clear blue day: I spoke again into the whirling void.

After the individual person had become a joke, after jokes became the innermost substance of persons, after the rain fell and dispersed the frost in cold eddies of water casting up mud and drowning the spores; after a wind rose up again and froze the outer scum of the pond and the rain that had fallen; after the electricity poles where the birds used to perch suddenly stood empty of both birds and wires; after a motorbike disturbed the dusk; after a knife pasted to a board of wood, covered with paint, suddenly flashed from inside the art work: the mind flashes, open to its own ground: the spiral motion empties itself again of all content—; after the stage collapses in the hilarity of its invention; after the geese fly shrieking through the barely intelligible sky and a potted plant is tipped over and dumps its soil on the always soggy carpet, one or two half-broken clods crumbling through a break in the screen, releasing one single crumb through the screen, into the outside world: the dead electricity poles fill with crows, the crows caw: she speaks into the spiral motion.

I spoke into the whirling void. After the privilege of the infinite turned out to be finite; after the mission of reading is felled by televised idols; when an extra step away from the desert road means to lose the road forever; after negation is called into question by a viscous goo of image that accumulates on everything, even on nothingness, especially on nothingness, until nothingness is goo; after the geese flew through a departing patch of orange sunlight: the glimmer of nothingness catches your eye from inside the spiral: it is possible to move again, into a new space, because of the split: the woods echo and crash in the throes of the tremor: the plates and glasses, the silverware, slide from the table—; after their crash, a great silence; after the great silence, a potential leaf pile; after the leaf-pile has been assembled and played in, its every audible crinkle savored and memorized and productive of new language in the aftermath, one that does not contain in it a word for "death" with the slightest negative connotation; then comes a spiral motion.

After amazed solitude solved its maze and became lonely, after golden eggs hatched into golden eaglets, after the sumptuous cradle grew too tiny to contain even the smallest of offspring, something smooth and pristine abandoning its own idea of itself for someone else's idea of it and becoming lumpy, after the dazzle of being and the razzle-dazzle of non-being; after a wax cast was slipped over a feverish living form, after the form in its fever melted all the wax and emerged from the drippings, even more feverish than before, glistening, distorted, human; when the guard barked at the visitor, mistaking him for a prisoner, and the visitor drew further into the cluster of inmates, until the guard, who would remain in the prison on a longer bid than the visitor or any of the inmates, realized his mistake and utterly altered his tone of voice, the voice suddenly the kind one human offers to another, the willed change of which was more horrific in its implications than the original snarl; after the ping-pong table, set outdoors, warps beyond the hope of predictable bounce and abandons all hope of garnering attention, beading with moss the color of its own paint, its aluminum legs buckling in submission to its pariah status; after the spongy terrain of syntax and forest floor becomes its own *raison d'etre*, dotted with barely perceptible trails along which the postman must walk if he wants to deliver the unretractable message; when the obscene word, shorn of any other way of being uttered except as an obscenity, or of being sent, except as an obscenity, sickens, gets ready to be said but then grows silent: for words on their own can never weep: the web is filled with living flies: long-forgotten wrecks tremble in their undersea graves, as if suddenly, in spite of all, they had expectations: the fish, swimming in spiraling schools around the ruined hulk, are agitated too, as if anticipating a sudden change: no wind, but all the pines along the shore-line bend slightly towards the bay: the reader tosses aside his book and walks away before anything happens, because nothing ever seems to really happen: the captain jettisons half-filled barrels in anticipation of a storm: the wanderer jettisons his rucksack and decides to stay put, where he has come. Of these three only the wanderer finds he must recant. He picks up his rucksack, spirals away.

There is no map. It is either a beach or a desert the wanderer traverses, or both at once. After the plovers nest has been raided and the plovers eggs have been eaten, after the walking dunes have buried the wanderers footprints and the tiny broken egg shells; after the wanderer has gone many miles along this strip of land either coastal or arid or perhaps both at once; after his wandering has become increasingly aimless and desperate:—every living being desires to wander and change, but this particular wanderer is already dead, having lost his argument with his lungs, recanted everything his heart has pumped, or so he feels as he wanders—; the ice-cube machine avalanches its creations into the bucket, the bucket is carried excitedly along the corridor back to the motel room, the cubes are dumped right away into the sink:—immediately upon coming to rest in the sink the ice begins to imperceptibly shift, those with ears discern a slight trickle of movement as beads of water begin to melt, to escape:—so the wanderer resting on his back in the soft sand feels his being indiscernibly trickle into the beach, or was it a desert, a ditch in the epistemic ground, grain upon grain of unique matter stamped to the outline of his body; after he had slept in that position for what seemed to him like an eternity; after he had wondered how such a sleep was possible, to descend to such depths and to be able to emerge from such depths, until he realized he was awake; after a brown regulation football was swept in by the waves and he realized that yes, here was the ocean, therefore this was definitely a beach, only possibly a desert; after the placebo of words had worn off, which is to say nothing had worn off because placebos never wear off, never having had an effect; after gathering himself up to watch the sun rise as if by some supreme effort of the will on the part of both the wanderer and the sun; after adjusting his black eye patch and tugging on his floppy black cap:—the sun rises over the sea:—men clamor for meaning, women clamor for freedom, children clamor for chump change:—in the gathering light, one of each lay in the hammock and shared a drink, passing the glass back and forth amongst themselves with some care: look, here come cows and horses being herded down the beach, or a spiral motion of sealed instructions, or a domestic camel mistaken for a wild camel: as if it was you was who was writing into this spiral void, the camel really wild and this a desert after all.

John Brown's Body

There is so little that is individual and just.
You would think we had never been bees and beekeepers
collaborating on honey.   In the hive of the subway
we glimpse guitar players singing sadly in Spanish.
Together on the couch the daughter laughs
and, outfitted in maiden speech, playfully
speaks the line: "read 'to be or not to be'
not the right way." At her father's behest she will squirt
the curvaceous woman in the playground who isn't yet
wet enough. Already she mouths the word "moldering,"
munches banana chips on the 2 train, meditates on colors.
The first guitar and the one not yet strung
tune themselves together, preparing a next song.
Like chinchillas, nipping mischievously
at fingers extended through the cage, highly American.
As in provoke something. Fight for the familiar things
the patriots only pretend to stand for. In Thoreau's words
Let your life be a counter-friction to stop the machine.
There is so little that is individual and just.